180 DAYS™ of Reading for Kindergarten

Author
Chandra Prough, M.S.Ed., NBCT

Program Credits

Corinne Burton, M.A.Ed., *President and Publisher*
Emily R. Smith, M.A.Ed., *SVP of Content Development*
Véronique Bos, *VP of Creative*
Lynette Ordoñez, *Content Manager*
Ashley Oberhaus, M.Ed., *Content Specialist*
Melissa Laughlin, *Editor*
David Slayton, *Assistant Editor*
Jill Malcolm, *Graphic Designer*

Image Credits: all images from Shutterstock and/or iStock

Standards

Shell Education
A division of Teacher Created Materials
5482 Argosy Avenue
Huntington Beach, CA 92649
www.tcmpub.com/shell-education
ISBN 979-8-7659-1802-9

Printed by: 590835
Printed in: China

Table of Contents

Introduction

180 Days of Practice

Appendix

Introduction

The Need for Practice

To be successful in today's reading classroom, students must deeply understand both concepts and procedures so that they can discuss and demonstrate their understanding. Demonstrating understanding is a process that must be continually practiced for students to be successful. According to Robert Marzano, "Practice has always been, and always will be, a necessary ingredient to learning procedural knowledge at a level at which students execute it independently" (2010, 83). Practice is especially important to help students apply reading comprehension strategies and word-study skills. *180 Days of Reading* offers teachers and parents a full page of reading comprehension and word recognition practice activities for each day of the school year.

The Science of Reading

For some people, reading comes easily. They barely remember how it happened. For others, learning to read takes more effort.

The goal of reading research is to understand the differences in how people learn to read and find the best ways to help all students learn. The term *Science of Reading* is commonly used to refer to this body of research. It helps people understand how to provide instruction in learning the code of the English language, how to develop fluency, and how to navigate challenging text and make sense of it.

Much of this research has been around for decades. In fact, in the late 1990s, Congress commissioned a review of the reading research. In 2000, the National Reading Panel (NRP) published a report that became the backbone of the Science of Reading. The NRP report highlights five components of effective reading instruction. These include the following:

- **Phonemic Awareness:** understanding and manipulating individual speech sounds
- **Phonics:** matching sounds to letters for use in reading and spelling
- **Fluency:** reading connected text accurately and smoothly
- **Vocabulary:** knowing the meanings of words in speech and in print
- **Reading Comprehension:** understanding what is read

There are two commonly referenced frameworks that build on reading research and provide a visual way for people to understand what is needed to learn to read. In the mid-1980s, a framework called the Simple View of Reading was introduced (Gough and Tunmer 1986). It shows that reading comprehension is possible when students are able to decode (or read) the words and have the language to understand the words.

The Simple View of Reading

Decoding × Language Comprehension = Reading Comprehension

Another framework that builds on the research behind the Science of Reading is Scarborough's Reading Rope (Scarborough 2001). It shows specific skills needed for both language comprehension and word recognition. The "strands" of the rope for language comprehension include having background content knowledge, knowing vocabulary, understanding language structure, having verbal reasoning, and understanding literacy. Word recognition includes phonological awareness, decoding skills, and sight recognition of familiar words (Scarborough 2001). As individual skills are strengthened and practiced, they become increasingly strategic and automatic to promote reading comprehension.

The Science of Reading *(cont.)*

Many parts of our understanding of how people learn to read stand the test of time and have been confirmed by more recent studies. However, new research continues to add to the understanding of reading. Some of this research shows the importance of wide reading (reading about a variety of topics), motivation, and self-regulation. The conversation will never be over, as new research will continue to refine the understanding of how people learn to read. There is always more to learn!

180 Days of Reading has been informed by this reading research. This series provides opportunities for students to practice the skills that years of research indicate contribute to reading growth. There are several features in this book that are supported by the Science of Reading.

Text Selection

- Carefully chosen texts offer experiences in a **wide range of text types**. Each unit includes fictional and nonfictional texts. They are presented in a variety of formats (e.g., poems, recipes, menus).
- Texts intentionally build upon one another to help students **build background knowledge** from day to day.
- Engaging with texts on the same topic for a thematic unit enables students to become familiar with related **vocabulary**, **language structure**, and **literacy knowledge**. This allows reading to become increasingly strategic and automatic, leading to better **fluency** and **comprehension**.

Activity Design

- Specific **language comprehension** and **word-recognition skills** are reinforced throughout the activities.
- Paired fiction and nonfiction texts are used to promote **comparison** and encourage students to **make connections** between texts within a unit.
- Students **write and draw to demonstrate understanding** of the texts.

This book provides the regular practice of reading skills that students need as they develop into excellent readers.

How to Use This Resource

Unit Structure Overview

This resource is organized into 18 units. Each two-week unit is organized in a consistent format for ease of use.

Week 1: Nonfiction

Day 1	Students read words and complete matching activities.
Day 2	Students read words and complete matching activities.
Day 3	Students listen to and read phrases and sentences and complete matching or circling activities.
Day 4	Students listen to and read nonfictional text and answer multiple-choice questions.
Day 5	Students reread the text from Day 4 and answer reading-response questions.

Week 2: Fiction

Day 1	Students read words and complete matching activities.
Day 2	Students read words and complete matching activities.
Day 3	Students listen to and read phrases and sentences and complete matching or circling activities.
Day 4	Students listen to and read fictional text and answer multiple-choice questions.
Day 5	Students reread the text from Day 4 and answer reading-response questions.

How to Use This Resource

Unit Structure Overview

Paired Texts

State standards have brought into focus the importance of preparing students for college and career success by expanding their critical thinking and analytical skills. It is no longer enough for students to read and comprehend a single text on a topic. Rather, the integration of ideas across texts is crucial for a more comprehensive understanding of themes presented by authors.

Literacy specialist Jennifer Soalt has written that paired text are "uniquely suited to scaffolding and extending students' comprehension" (2005, 680). She identifies three ways in which paired fictional and nonfictional texts are particularly effective in increasing comprehension: through the building of background knowledge, the development of vocabulary, and the increase in student motivation (Soalt, 2005).

Each two-week unit in *180 Days of Reading for Kindergarten* is connected by a common theme or topic. Packets of each week's or each unit's practice pages can be prepared for students.

During Week 1, students read nonfictional texts and answer questions.

During Week 2, students read fictional texts and answer questions.

How to Use This Resource

Student Practice Pages

Practice pages reinforce grade-level skills across a variety of foundational reading concepts for each day of year. The questions are provided as full practice pages, making them easy to prepare and implement as part of a morning routine, at the beginning of each reading lesson, or as homework.

Days 1–3

Days 1 and 2 of each week follow a consistent format, with matching activities for single words.

Tracing lines are provided in earlier units to support emergent readers.

Name: Date:
Unit 1 WEEK 1 DAY 1
Directions: Match the words to the pictures.
bag wag tag
1. tag
2. bag
3. wag
Directions: Circle the word for the picture. Write the word.
4. rag sag
rag
© Shell Education 135042—180 Days of Reading

Unit 1 WEEK 1 DAY 2
Name: Date:
Directions: Match the words to the pictures.
fan man tan
1. man
2. tan
3. fan
Directions: Circle the word for the picture. Write the word.
4. van can
can
12 © Shell Education 135042—180 Days of Reading

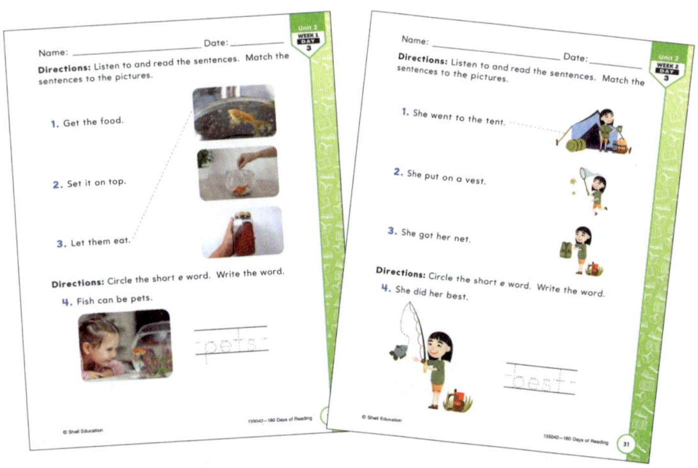
Name: Date:
Unit 2 WEEK 1 DAY 3
Directions: Listen to and read the sentences. Match the sentences to the pictures.
1. Get the food.
2. Set it on top.
3. Let them eat.
Directions: Circle the short e word. Write the word.
4. Fish can be pets.
pets
© Shell Education 135042—180 Days of Reading

Name: Date:
Unit 2 WEEK 2 DAY 3
Directions: Listen to and read the sentences. Match the sentences to the pictures.
1. She went to the tent.
2. She put on a vest.
3. She got her net.
Directions: Circle the short e word. Write the word.
4. She did her best.
best
© Shell Education 135042—180 Days of Reading 31

Day 3 of each week follows a consistent format, with matching and circling activities for phrases and sentences.

How to Use This Resource

Student Practice Pages *(cont.)*

Days 4–5

Days 4 and 5 of each week follow a consistent format, with a longer text and full-color illustrations.

Unit 2 WEEK 3 DAY 4–5

Name: Date:

Pet Fish

Fish can be pets. Fish need to be wet. Put them in a fish tank. Put the tank on a desk.

The water will be fresh. The tank can have a shell. It can have a wreck.

Fish need to be fed. Get the food. Set it on top. Let them eat.

Unit 2 WEEK 3 DAY 4–5

Name: Date:

Meg Gets to Fish

Meg went to the tent.

She put on a vest.

She got her net.

She did her best to get fish.

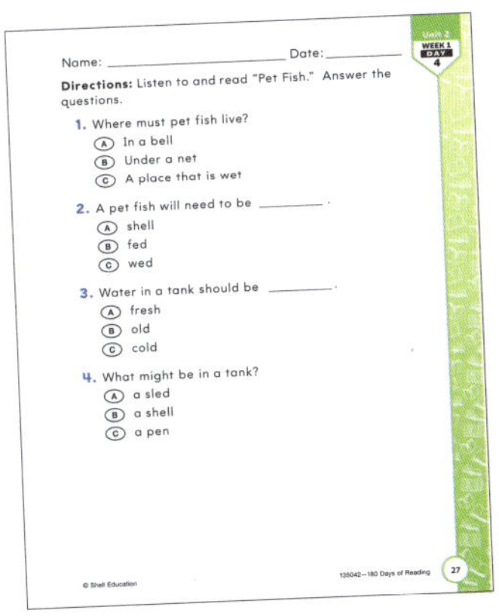
Name: Date:

Directions: Listen to and read "Pet Fish." Answer the questions.

1. Where must pet fish live?
   - Ⓐ In a bell
   - Ⓑ Under a net
   - Ⓒ A place that is wet
2. A pet fish will need to be _____.
   - Ⓐ shell
   - Ⓑ fed
   - Ⓒ wed
3. Water in a tank should be _____.
   - Ⓐ fresh
   - Ⓑ old
   - Ⓒ cold
4. What might be in a tank?
   - Ⓐ a sled
   - Ⓑ a shell
   - Ⓒ a pen

On day 4, students answer multiple-choice questions focused on reading comprehension.

On day 5, students use words and pictures to respond to reading-response prompts.

Name: Date:

Directions: Listen to and read the story "Meg Gets to Fish" again. What happens next? Finish the story with a picture. Label the picture.

Instructional Options

180 Days of Reading is a flexible resource that can be used in various instructional settings for different purposes.

- Use these student pages as daily warm-up activities or as review.
- Work with students in small groups, allowing them to focus on specific skills. This setting also lends itself to partner and group discussions about the texts.
- Student pages in this resource can be completed during center times and as activities for early finishers.

How to Use This Resource *(cont.)*

Diagnostic Assessment

The practice pages in this book can be used as diagnostic assessments. These activity pages require students to think critically, respond to questions, and identify words. (An answer key for the practice pages is provided starting on page 230.)

For each unit, analysis sheets are provided as *Microsoft Word®* files in the digital resources. There is a *Class Analysis Sheet* and an *Individual Analysis Sheet*. Use the file that matches your assessment needs. After each week, record how many answers each student got correct on the unit's analysis sheet. Only record the answers for Days 1–4. The Day 5 activities can be evaluated using the writing rubric or other evaluation tools (see below). At the end of each unit, analyze the data on the analysis sheet to determine instructional focuses for your child or class.

The diagnostic analysis tools included in the digital resources allow for quick evaluation and ongoing monitoring of student work. See at a glance which reading genre students may need to focus on further to develop proficiency.

Using the Results to Differentiate Instruction

Once results are gathered and analyzed, use the data to inform the way to differentiate instruction. The data can help determine which concepts are the most difficult for students and that need additional instructional support and continued practice.

The results of the diagnostic analysis may show that an entire class is struggling with a particular genre or letter pattern. If these concepts have been taught in the past, this indicates that further instruction or reteaching is necessary. If these concepts have not been taught yet, this data is a great preassessment and demonstrates that students do not have a working knowledge of the concepts.

The results of the diagnostic analysis may also show that an individual or small group of students is struggling with a particular concept or group of concepts. Consider pulling aside these students while others are working independently to instruct further on the concept(s). You can also use the results to help identify individuals or groups of proficient students who are ready for enrichment or above-grade-level instruction. These students may benefit from independent learning contracts or more challenging activities.

Writing Rubric

A rubric for Day 5 activities is provided on page 229. Review and discuss the rubric with students. Score students' responses, and provide them with feedback on their writing.

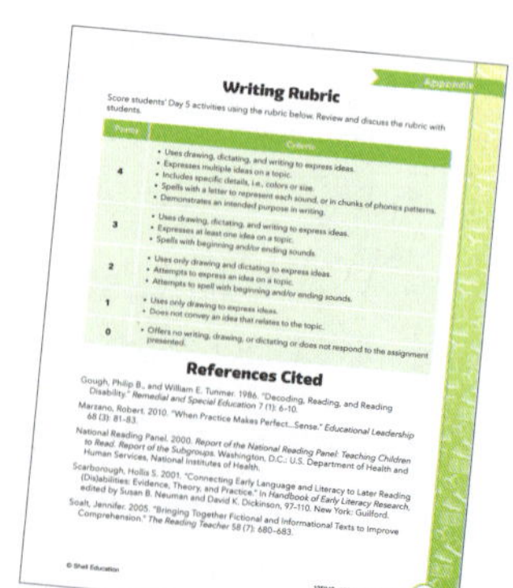

Name: ______________________ Date: ____________

Directions: Match the words to the pictures.

bag

wag

tag

1. tag

2. bag

3. wag

Directions: Circle the word for the picture. Write the word.

4.

rag sag

____

rag

Name: ______________________ Date: ____________

Directions: Match the words to the pictures.

fan

man

tan

1. man

2. tan

3. fan

Directions: Circle the word for the picture. Write the word.

4.

van can

____

can

Name: ______________________ Date: __________

Directions: Listen to and read the sentences. Circle the short *a* words

1. The bat sat.

2. A bat can fly.

3. It has a fang.

Directions: Circle the short *a* word. Write the word.

4. Look at it hang.

at

Name: ______________________ Date: ____________

A Bat

This is a bat.

This is a bat fang.

This is a bat wing.

This is a bat ear.

A bat can be black. A bat can be tan.

A bat can fly. A bat can land. A bat can hang.

Name: ______________________________ Date: ____________

Directions: Listen to and read "A Bat." Answer the questions.

1. What can a bat do?
   - (A) drive a van
   - (B) fly
   - (C) wear pants

2. What is this?

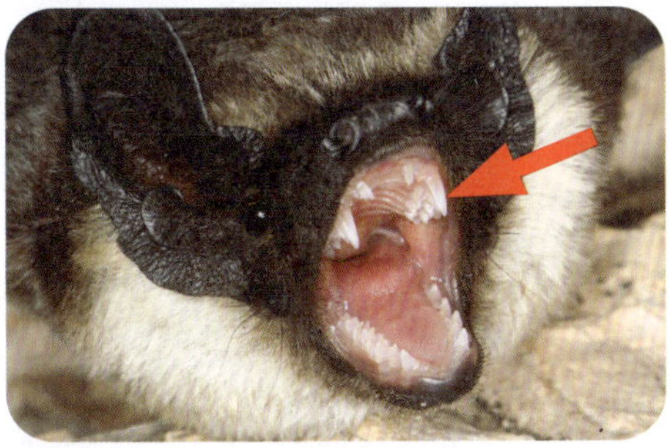

   - (A) a fang
   - (B) a hat
   - (C) a wing

3. A bat can be ________.
   - (A) black
   - (B) purple
   - (C) pink

4. Which is another good title?
   - (A) A Bat and a Dad
   - (B) In the Trash
   - (C) All about Bats

Name: ______________________________ Date: ____________

Directions: Listen to and read "A Bat" again. Draw a bat. Circle the parts of a bat in your drawing.

Parts of a Bat

fang wing ear

Name: ______________________________ Date: ____________

Directions: Match the words to the pictures.

cat

bat

sat

1. sat

2. bat

3. cat

Directions: Circle the word for the picture. Write the word.

4. 

rat hat

rat

Name: ______________________ Date: ____________

Directions: Match the words to the pictures.

hat

pat

cat

1. pat 

2. hat 

3. cat 

Directions: Circle the word for the picture. Write the word.

4. 

cat   mat

mat

Name: ______________________________ Date: ____________

Directions: Listen to and read the sentences. Match the sentences to the pictures.

1. The man sat.

2. The cat sat.

3. The bat sat.

Directions: Circle the short *a* word. Write the word.

4. The dog ran.

____

ran

Name: ______________________ Date: ____________

The Bat and the Rat

A bat sat.

A rat sat.

A man saw them.

Oh no! A bat and a rat!

Name: ______________________ Date: __________

Directions: Listen to and read "The Bat and the Rat." Answer the questions.

1. Who sees the bat?
   - (A) a cat
   - (B) Dan
   - (C) a man

2. What does the rat do?
   - (A) run
   - (B) sit
   - (C) jab

3. Why is the man surprised?
   - (A) He does not like the bat and the rat.
   - (B) He likes the bat and rat.
   - (C) He does not like the mat and the man.

4. Which is another good title?
   - (A) On the Mat
   - (B) A Big Surprise
   - (C) A Man

Name: ______________________________ Date: ____________

Directions: Listen to and read "The Bat and the Rat." What happens next? Finish the story with a picture. Label the picture.

____

Name: ______________________ Date: ____________

Directions: Match the words to the pictures.

pet

vet

wet

1. wet

2. vet

3. pet

Directions: Circle the word for the picture. Write the word.

4.

set net

net

Name: ______________________ Date: __________

Directions: Match the words to the pictures.

fed

bed

desk

1. desk

2. fed

3. bed

Directions: Circle the word for the picture. Write the word.

4. 

wreck bed

____

wreck

Name: ______________________ Date: ____________

Directions: Listen to and read the sentences. Match the sentences to the pictures.

1. Get the food.

2. Set it on top.

3. Let them eat.

Directions: Circle the short *e* word. Write the word.

4. Fish can be pets.

pets

Name: ______________________ Date: ____________

Pet Fish

Fish can be pets. Fish need to be wet. Put them in a fish tank. Put the tank on a desk.

The water will be fresh. The tank can have a shell. It can have a wreck.

Fish need to be fed. Get the food. Set it on top. Let them eat.

Name: ______________________________ Date: ____________

Directions: Listen to and read "Pet Fish." Answer the questions.

1. Where must pet fish live?
   - (A) in a bell
   - (B) under a net
   - (C) a place that is wet

2. Pet fish need to be ________.
   - (A) shell
   - (B) fed
   - (C) wed

3. Water in a tank should be ________.
   - (A) fresh
   - (B) old
   - (C) dirty

4. What might be in a tank?
   - (A) a sled
   - (B) a shell
   - (C) a pen

Name: ______________________ Date: ____________

Directions: Listen to and read "Pet Fish" again. Draw what you might see in a fish tank.

Name: ______________________________ Date: ____________

Directions: Match the words to the pictures.

peg

beg

Meg

1. beg
2. peg
3. Meg

Directions: Circle the word for the picture. Write the word.

4.

leg   peg

leg

Name: ______________________ Date: __________

Directions: Match the words to the pictures.

bell

fell

yell

1. yell

2. bell

3. fell

Directions: Circle the word for the picture. Write the word.

4.

well tell

well

Name: ______________________ Date: ____________

Directions: Listen to and read the sentences. Match the sentences to the pictures.

1. She went to the tent.

2. She put on a vest.

3. She got her net.

Directions: Circle the short *e* word. Write the word.

4. She did her best.

best

Name: ______________________ Date: ____________

Meg Gets to Fish

Meg went to the tent.

She put on a vest.

She got her net.

She did her best to get fish.

Name: ______________________ Date: ____________

Directions: Listen to and read "Meg Gets to Fish." Answer the questions.

1. Who will go fishing?
   - (A) Meg
   - (B) the net
   - (C) the tent

2. Where does Meg get her vest?
   - (A) at home
   - (B) in a tent
   - (C) at school

3. How will Meg get the fish?
   - (A) with her vest
   - (B) with the net
   - (C) with her tent

4. Which is another good title?
   - (A) Lose a Vest
   - (B) Fix a Net
   - (C) Set to Fish

Name: ______________________ Date: __________

Directions: Listen to and read "Meg Gets to Fish" again. What happens next? Finish the story with a picture. Label the picture.

____

Name: ______________________ Date: __________

Directions: Match the words to the pictures.

big

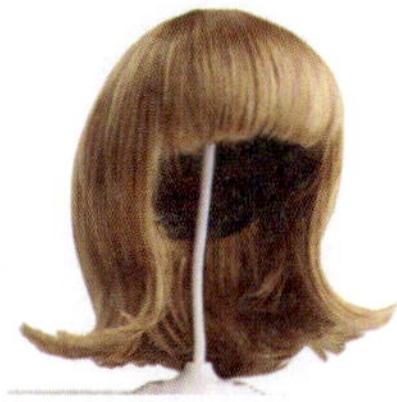
wig

rig

1. rig 

2. wig ------------------ 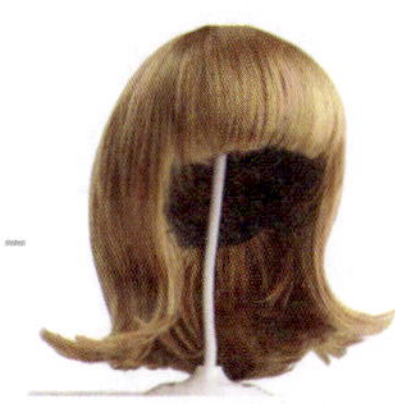

3. big 

Directions: Circle the word for the picture. Write the word.

4. 

wig jig

jig

Name: ______________________ Date: ____________

Directions: Match the words to the pictures.

dip

chip

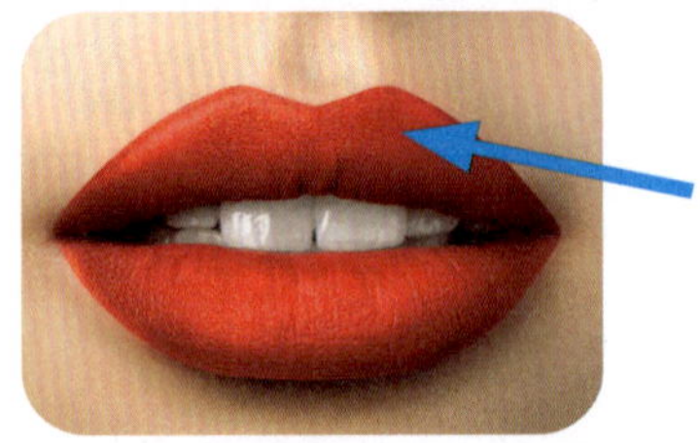
lip

1. lip

2. dip

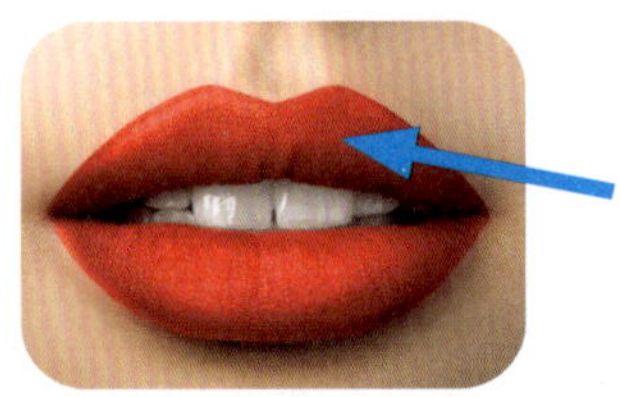

3. chip

Directions: Circle the word for the picture. Write the word.

4. 

drip lip

drip

Name: ______________________________ Date: ____________

Directions: Listen to and read the sentences. Circle the short *i* words.

1. A rig can dig.

2. A dog can dig a pit.

3. Which do you pick to dig?

Directions: Circle the short *i* word. Write the word.

4. What do you see the pig do?

pig

Name: ______________________ Date: ____________

Things That Dig

A rig can dig.
It can dig a big pit.

A dog can dig.
It can dig with its paws.

This can help dig.
It can help lift the dirt.

A worm can dig.
It digs inch by inch.

A kid can dig.
She can dig with a pick.

Name: ______________________ Date: ____________

Directions: Listen to and read "Things that Dig." Answer the questions.

1. This text is about ________.
   - (A) animals
   - (B) kinds of holes
   - (C) things that dig

2. What does the kid use to dig?
   - (A) a spoon
   - (B) a pick
   - (C) her hands

3. Which would you use to dig a big pit?
   - (A) a rig
   - (B) a dog
   - (C) a fork

4. What does a dog use to dig?
   - (A) a ring
   - (B) its paws
   - (C) its lip

Unit 3
WEEK 1
DAY
5

Name: ______________________ Date: __________

Directions: Listen to and read "Things that Dig" again. Look at the pictures. Write what the text is about. Then, draw yourself digging.

The text is about things that dig.

Name: ______________________ Date: ____________

Directions: Match the words to the pictures.

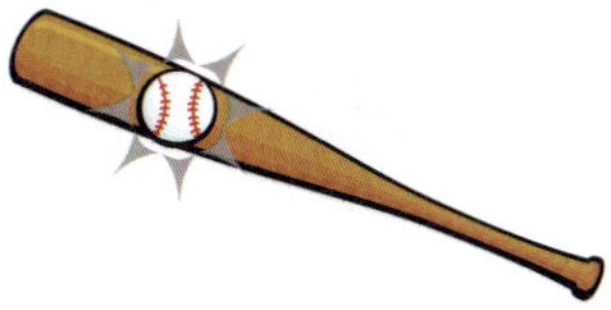
hit

him

hid

1. hid 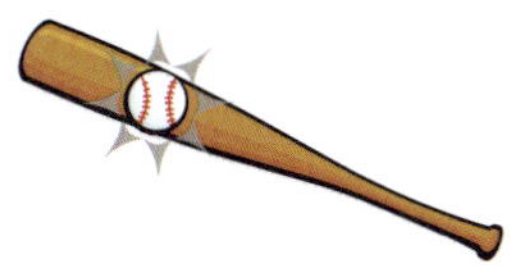

2. him - - - - - - - - - - - - - - - - - - 

3. hit 

Directions: Circle the word for the picture. Write the word.

4.

hip hid

hip

Name: ______________________________ Date: ____________

Directions: Match the words to the pictures.

pick

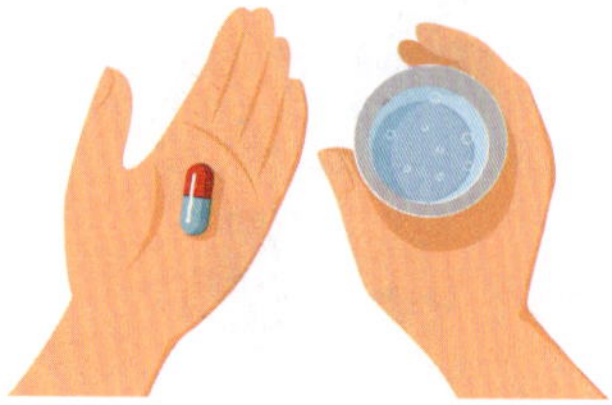
pill

pit

1. pick 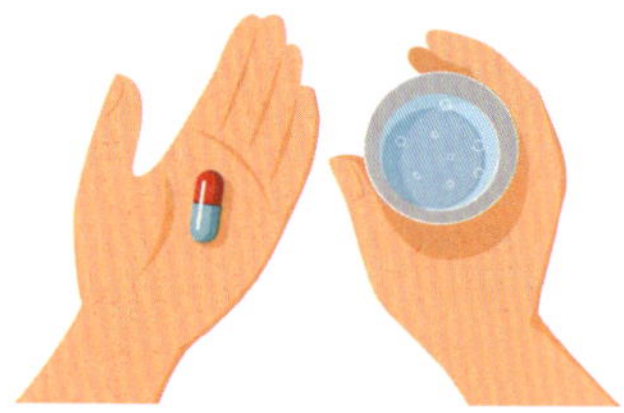

2. pill 

3. pit - 

Directions: Circle the word for the picture. Write the word.

4.

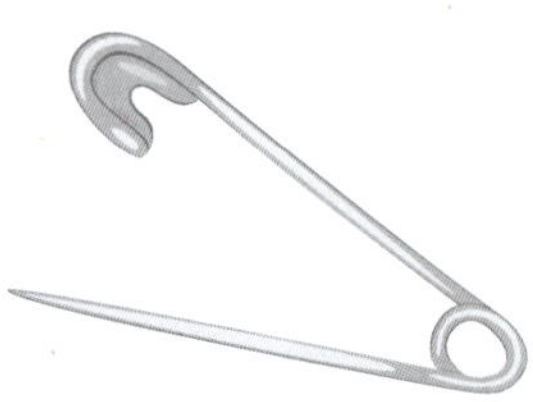

pit pin

____

pin

Name: ______________________ Date: ____________

Directions: Listen to and read the sentences. Circle the short *i* words.

1. Cats like to dig.

2. What a stink!

3. He hid in the sink.

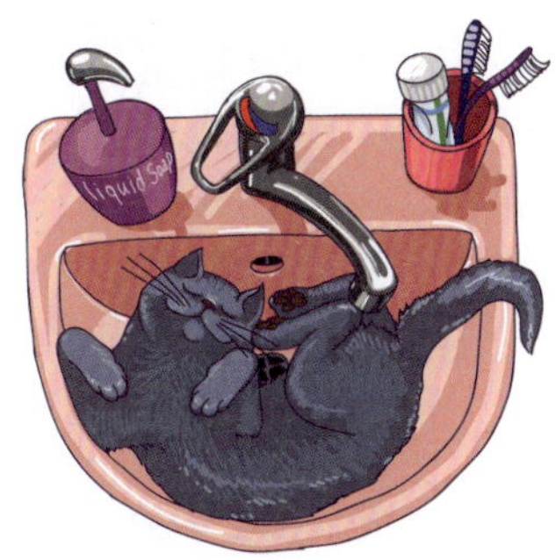

Directions: Circle the word for the picture. Write the word.

4\.

sink kiss

kiss

Name: ______________________________ Date: ____________

Pib Likes to Dig

Pib likes to dig.

He digs in the bin.

Get him out of the bin!

Kim puts Pib in the sink.

Meow!

Name: ______________________ Date: ____________

Directions: Listen to and read "Pib Likes to Dig." Answer the questions.

1. Who likes to dig?
   - (A) Pib
   - (B) Kim
   - (C) the bin

2. Where does Pib dig?
   - (A) out of the bin
   - (B) in the bin
   - (C) with Kim

3. Why does Kim put Pib in the sink?
   - (A) Pib gets dirty.
   - (B) Pib wants to drink.
   - (C) Pib wants to dig.

4. Which is another good title?
   - (A) Kim Likes to Dig
   - (B) Messy Cat
   - (C) Messy Kim

Name: ______________________ Date: ____________

Directions: Listen to and read "Pib Likes to Dig" again. What happens next? Finish the story with a picture. Label the picture.

Name: ______________________________ Date: ____________

Directions: Match the words to the pictures.

dog

jog

hog

1. hog -

2. dog

3. jog

Directions: Circle the word for the picture. Write the word.

4.

fog   log

log

Name: ______________________ Date: ____________

Directions: Match the words to the pictures.

blob

cob

knob

1. knob
2. cob
3. blob

Directions: Circle the word for the picture. Write the word.

4. 

job   mob

job

Name: ______________________ Date: __________

Directions: Listen to and read the sentences. Match the sentences to the pictures.

1. Turn the stove to hot.

2. Shake the pot.

3. Wait for them to pop.

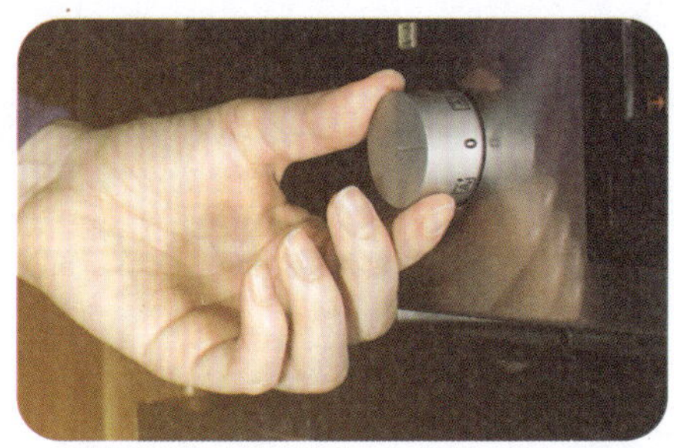

Directions: Trace the word. Circle the picture of the word.

4.

stove

Name: ______________________ Date: ____________

How to Make Corn Pop

What to Get

pot with a top

corn

oil

salt

Steps

1. Put a pot on the stove.
2. Add a bit of this. 
3. Add this. 
4. Turn the stove to hot. Add the top.
5. Shake the pot.
6. Wait for the pops to stop.
7. Toss with some of this. 

Name: ______________________________ Date: ____________

Directions: Listen to and read "How to Make Corn Pop." Answer the questions.

1. The author wrote the words to ________.
   - (A) make you laugh
   - (B) make you sing
   - (C) teach you

2. The pictures help you ________.
   - (A) make popcorn
   - (B) sing a song
   - (C) put on your sock

3. What do you need to make corn pop?
   - (A) a glove
   - (B) a pot
   - (C) a sock

4. Which is another good title?
   - (A) Go for a Jog
   - (B) How to Make Popcorn
   - (C) Pop and the Dog

Name: ______________________ Date: ____________

Directions: Listen to and read "How to Make Corn Pop" again. What happens next? Draw a picture. Label the picture.

Name: ______________________________ Date: ____________

Directions: Match the words to the pictures.

mop

top

pop

1. top

2. mop

3. pop

Directions: Circle the word for the picture. Write the word.

4.

cop hop

hop

Name: ______________________________ Date: ______________

Directions: Match the words to the pictures.

cot

dot

hot

1. hot

2. cot

3. dot

Directions: Circle the word for the picture. Write the word.

4.

lot pot

pot

Name: ______________________ Date: ____________

Directions: Listen to and read the sentences. Match the sentences to the pictures.

1. He got a mop.

2. This is corn on the cob.

3. The pot is hot.

Directions: Circle the short *o* word. Write the word.

4. His hat is up top.

top

Name: ______________________ Date: ____________

Bob's Hot Pot

Bob got a pot hot.

He put in corn to pop.

He did not put on a top.

Bob got a mop.

Name: ______________________________ Date: ____________

Directions: Listen to and read "Bob's Hot Pot." Answer the questions.

1. What does Bob put in the pot?
   - (A) a hot top
   - (B) a hot sock
   - (C) corn to pop

2. What does Bob **not** do?
   - (A) put on a top
   - (B) put in the corn
   - (C) get the pot hot

3. What does Bob do to the pot?
   - (A) get a top
   - (B) get it hot
   - (C) get a mop

4. What is Bob's job?
   - (A) to mop up
   - (B) to get the corn hotter
   - (C) to make a mess

Name: ______________________________ Date: ____________

Directions: Listen to and read "Bob's Hot Pot" again. What does Bob do with the mop? Finish the story with a picture. Label the picture.

Name: ______________________________ Date: ____________

Directions: Match the words to the pictures.

jug

rug

dug

1. dug

2. rug

3. jug

Directions: Circle the word for the picture. Write the word.

4.

bug hug

____

Name: ______________________ Date: ____________

Directions: Match the words to the pictures.

cub

sub

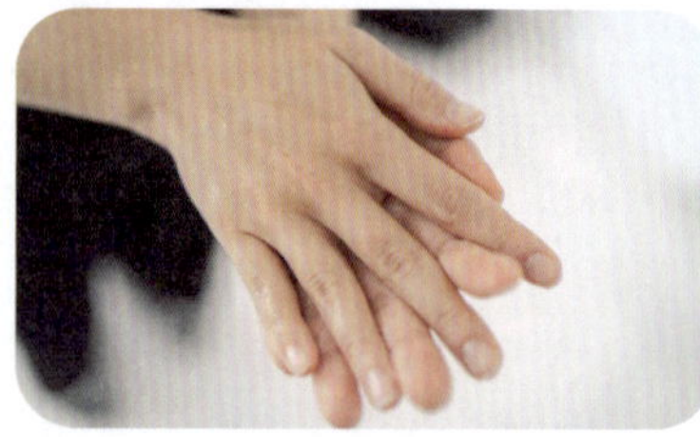

rub

1. sub

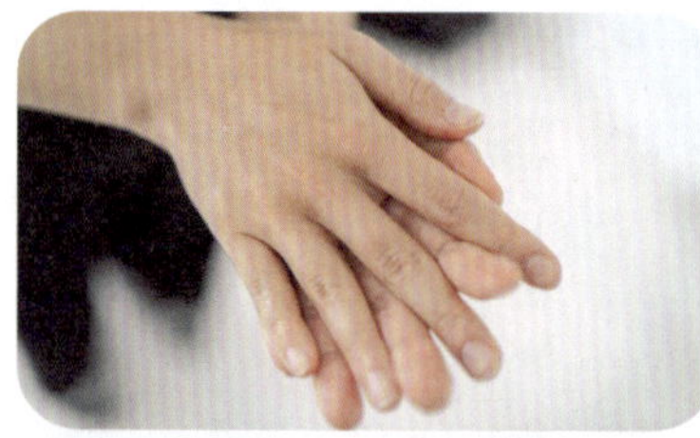

2. rub

3. cub

Directions: Circle the word for the picture. Write the word.

4. 

hub tub

Name: ______________________ Date: __________

Directions: Listen to and read the sentences. Match the sentences to the pictures.

1. A baby dog is a pup.

2. A baby bat is a pup.

3. A baby bear is a cub.

Directions: Circle the short *u* word. Write the word.

4. A baby fox is a cub.

____

Name: ______________________ Date: ____________

Pups and Cubs

dog

A pup is a baby dog.

bat

A pup is a baby bat.

bear

A cub is a baby bear.

fox

A cub is a baby fox.

Name: ______________________________ Date: ____________

Directions: Listen to and read "Pups and Cubs." Answer the questions.

1. What is a pup?
   - (A) a baby bear
   - (B) a baby dog
   - (C) a baby bird

2. What is a cub?
   - (A) a baby bear
   - (B) a baby dog
   - (C) a baby cow

3. Which would make the best pet?
   - (A) a bat
   - (B) a bear
   - (C) a dog

4. Which is another good title?
   - (A) Dogs
   - (B) Bears
   - (C) Baby Animals

Name: ______________________ Date: ____________

Directions: Listen to and read "Pups and Cubs" again. Look at the animals. Choose one pup and one cub to add to the text.

Pups

wolf 

mouse 

shark 

Cubs

panda 

cheetah 

tiger 

A baby ______________________ is a pup, too.

A baby ______________________ is a cub, too.

Name: ______________________ Date: ____________

Directions: Match the words to the pictures.

cup

cud

cub

1. cup 

2. cub 

3. cud 

Directions: Circle the word for the picture. Write the word.

4. 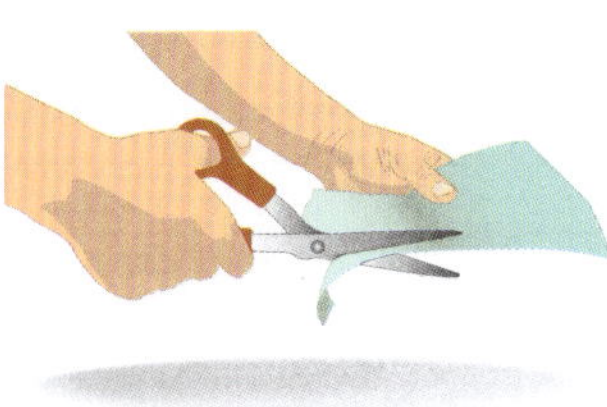

cup cut

____

Name: ______________________ Date: ____________

Directions: Match the words to the pictures.

hug

huff

hum

1. huff

2. hum

3. hug

Directions: Circle the word for the picture. Write the word.

4.

hull hut

____

Name: ______________________ Date: __________

Directions: Listen to and read the sentences. Match the sentences to the pictures.

1. Gus can run.

2. Gus can jump.

3. Gus can brush.

Directions: Circle the short *u* word. Write the word.

4. He ate a nut.

____

Name: ______________________ Date: ____________

Gus and His Pets

Gus has two pets.

Gus can run and jump with one pet.

Ruff! Ruff!

One pet does not run or jump.

Quack! Quack!

Gus has fun with his pets.

Name: ______________________ Date: ____________

Directions: Listen to and read "Gus and His Pets." Answer the questions.

1. Who has pets?
   - (A) a pup
   - (B) a duck
   - (C) Gus

2. Which pet runs?
   - (A) a pup
   - (B) a duck
   - (C) a bird

3. What kinds of pets does Gus have?
   - (A) a pup and a duck
   - (B) a bug and a pup
   - (C) a duck and a cat

4. Which is another good title?
   - (A) Duck in the Pond
   - (B) Two Pets
   - (C) Gus Quacks

Name: ______________________ Date: __________

Directions: Listen to and read "Gus and His Pets" again. What happens next? Draw a picture. Label your picture.

Name: ______________________ Date: ____________

Directions: Match the words to the pictures.

key

kid

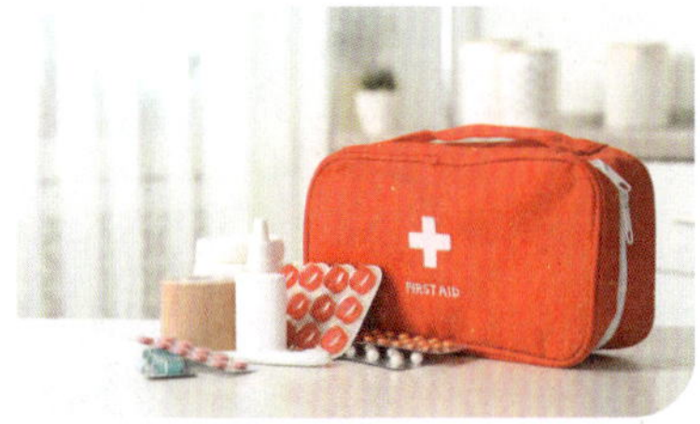
kit

1. kit

2. key

3. kid

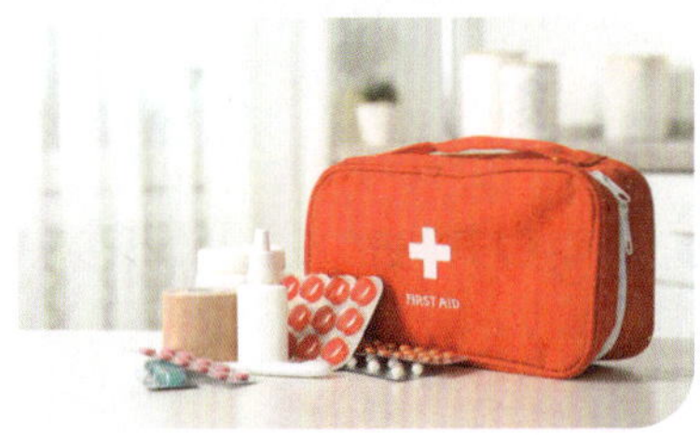

Directions: Circle the word for the picture. Write the word.

4.

king kiss

____

Name: ______________________________ Date: ____________

Directions: Match the words to the pictures.

good

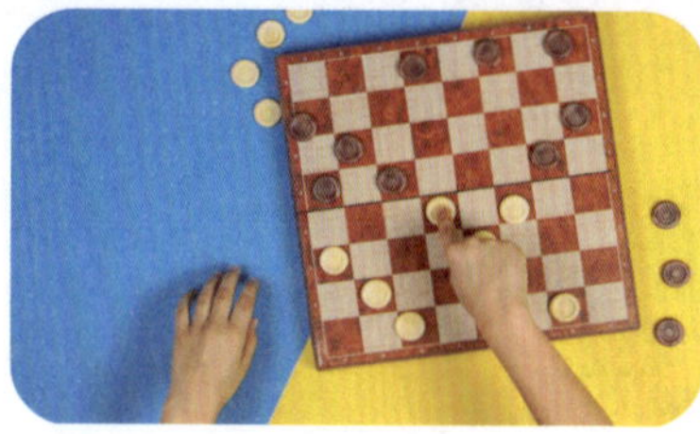

game

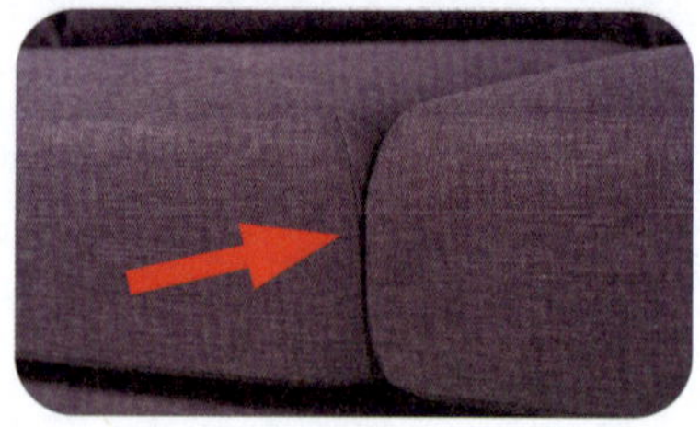

gap

1. gap

2. good

3. game

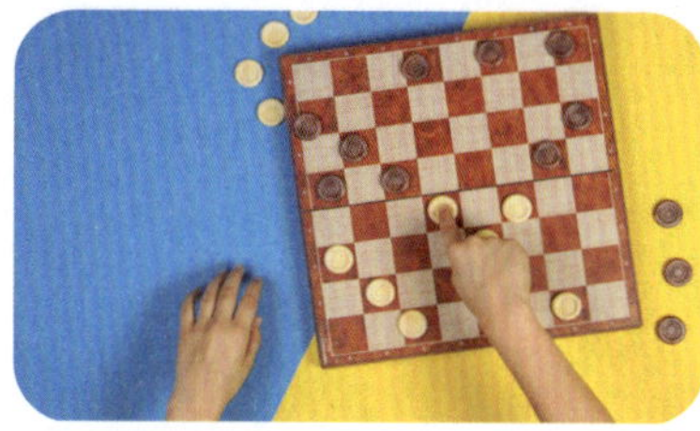

Directions: Circle the word for the picture. Write the word.

4.

goat game

____

Name: ______________________ Date: __________

Directions: Listen to and read the sentences. Match the sentences to the pictures.

1. Tap him to tag.

2. The other kids will run fast.

3. He will freeze.

Directions: Trace the word. Look at the picture. Circle the picture that goes with the word.

4. You can freeze it.

Name: ______________________ Date: ____________

Freeze Tag

Here is a new game.

First, get lots of kids. It will be fun for all.

One kid will be "it."

The rest of the kids will run fast.

The kid who is "it" will try to tag.

The kid who is tagged will freeze.

The kid will be still.

The game ends if all the kids get tagged. They will all freeze.

It is a good game!

Name: ______________________ Date: ____________

Directions: Listen to and read "Freeze Tag." Answer the questions.

1. How does freeze tag end?
   - (A) All kids get tagged.
   - (B) No kids get tagged.
   - (C) One kid will be "it."

2. What does it mean to *freeze*?
   - (A) lift your leg
   - (B) be still
   - (C) run fast

3. Why should you get lots of kids to play freeze tag?
   - (A) It is hard to play.
   - (B) It is fun for all.
   - (C) It is not nice.

4. What is this text about?
   - (A) a book in a bag
   - (B) how to play freeze tag
   - (C) sitting still

Name: ______________________ Date: ____________

Directions: Listen to and read "Freeze Tag" again. Think about how to play. Draw what happens after a kid gets tagged. Label your picture.

Name: ______________________ Date: ____________

Directions: Match the words to the pictures.

tap

tip

top

1. top 

2. tap 

3. tip 

Directions: Circle the word for the picture. Write the word.

4. 

tag tan

____

Name: ______________________ Date: ____________

Directions: Match the words to the pictures.

bat

bit

bet

1. bat

2. bet

3. bit

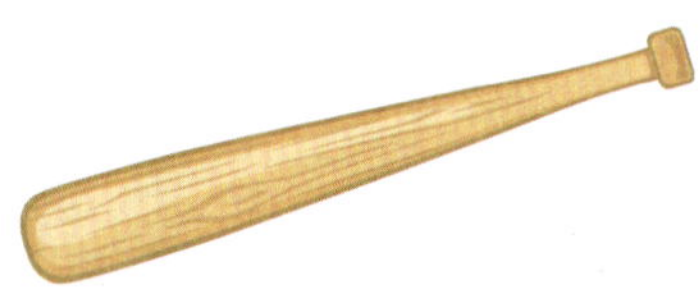

Directions: Circle the word for the picture. Write the word.

4.

Ben bug

____

Name: ______________________ Date: ____________

Directions: Listen to and read the sentences. Match the sentences to the pictures.

1. Pam and Sam play tag.

2. Pam ran fast.

3. Pam can tap Sam.

Directions: Circle the two words that start with *t*. Write the words.

4. In tag, you tap.

Name: ______________________ Date: ____________

Play Tag

tag

Pam and Sam play tag.

ran

Pam ran fast.

tap

Pam can tap Sam.

Sam

Sam is "it"!

Name: ______________________ Date: __________

Directions: Listen to and read "Play Tag." Answer the questions.

1. Who plays tag?
   - (A) Pam
   - (B) Sam
   - (C) Pam and Sam

2. Who runs fast?
   - (A) Sam
   - (B) Pam
   - (C) Pam and Sam

3. Why is Sam "it"?
   - (A) Pam ran fast.
   - (B) Pam taps Sam.
   - (C) Sam plays tag.

4. What is this story about?
   - (A) playing tag
   - (B) Sam
   - (C) standing still

Name: ______________________ Date: ____________

Directions: Listen to and read "Play Tag" again. What happens next? Draw a picture. Label your picture.

Name: ______________________________ Date: ____________

Directions: Match the words to the pictures.

pig

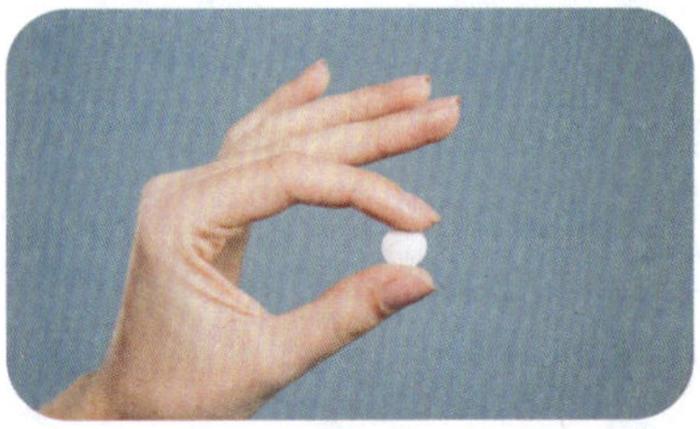

pill

pan

1. pig

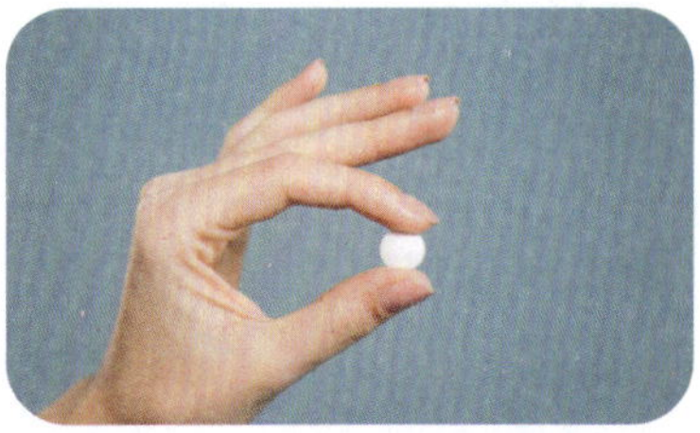

2. pan

3. pill

Directions: Circle the word for the picture. Write the word.

4.

pan paw

____

Name: ______________________ Date: ____________

Directions: Match the words to the pictures.

mud

man

mug

1. mug

2. mud

3. man

Directions: Circle the word for the picture. Write the word.

4. 

make   mail

Name: ______________________ Date: __________

Directions: Match the sentences to the pictures.

1. Pigs can live in pens.

2. Pigs like mud on a hot day.

3. Pigs can be pets.

Directions: Circle the words that start with *r*. Write the words.

4. Look at the pig run on the rug.

____

____

Name: ______________________ Date: __________

Facts about Pigs

Pigs can be good pets. Pigs can live in large pens.

Pigs get in mud on a hot day. It is how they stay cool.

Pigs are smart. Pigs eat all kinds of food.

They can dig. They can squeal!

Name: ______________________________ Date: ____________

Directions: Listen to and read "Facts about Pigs." Answer the questions.

1. Where can pigs live?
   - (A) in a house
   - (B) in large pens
   - (C) in cars

2. Which can pigs do?
   - (A) dig
   - (B) sing
   - (C) dance

3. Why do pigs get in mud?
   - (A) to eat food
   - (B) to take a nap
   - (C) to stay cool

4. Which is another good title?
   - (A) All about Pigs
   - (B) Why Pigs Don't Like Mud
   - (C) Don't Get a Pet Pig

Name: ______________________________ Date: ____________

Directions: Listen to and read "Facts about Pigs" again. Choose one fact. Draw a picture to show what it means.

Name: ______________________ Date: __________

Directions: Match the words to the pictures.

late

lock

lick

1. lick

2. late

3. lock

Directions: Circle the word for the picture. Write the word.

4.

light lip

____

Name: ______________________ Date: __________

Directions: Match the words to the pictures.

dot

dock

dog

1. dock 

2. dot 

3. dog 

Directions: Circle the word for the picture. Write the word.

4.

dice dug

____

Name: ______________________ Date: __________

Directions: Match the sentences to the pictures.

1. Pip the pig is on the run.

2. Mom was late to lock the gate.

3. She made a jump over Jill.

Directions: Circle the words that begin with *d*. Write the words.

4. She ran fast past the dog in the den.

____

____

Name: ______________________________ Date: ____________

Lock the Gate

Pip the pig is on the run.

Mom was late to lock the gate. Pip got out.

She did a big jump past Jill and Jane.

She ran fast past Dan and the dog in the den.

Pip wanted to lie by the log.

Name: ______________________ Date: ____________

Directions: Listen to and read "Lock the Gate." Answer the questions.

1. What is the story about?
   - (A) a pig in a pen
   - (B) a pig on the run
   - (C) a dog in a den

2. Why doesn't mom lock the gate?
   - (A) Dan is in the den.
   - (B) Jill goes for a jog.
   - (C) She is late.

3. What kind of animal is Pip?
   - (A) a cow
   - (B) a pig
   - (C) a dog

4. Which is another good title?
   - (A) Pip Gets Out
   - (B) Mom and Meg
   - (C) Get the Goat

Name: ______________________________ Date: _____________

Directions: Listen to and read "Lock the Gate" again. What might have happened if mom locked the gate? Draw and label a picture.

Name: ______________________ Date: ____________

Directions: Match the words to the pictures.

star

stripe

fast

1. fast

2. star

3. stripe

Directions: Circle the word for the picture. Write the word.

4. 

dust fist

____

Name: ______________________ Date: ____________

Directions: Match the words to the pictures.

sky

desk

skip

1. sky

2. skip

3. desk

Directions: Circle the word for the picture. Write the word.

4.

mask skunk

____

Name: ______________________ Date: __________

Directions: Listen to and read the sentences. Match the sentences to the pictures.

1. The flag has stars and stripes.

2. He learns at a desk.

3. The kid can skip.

Directions: Circle the word for the picture. Write the word.

4.

star stripe

____

Name: ______________________ Date: ____________

The U.S. Flag

Have you seen a flag in the sky?

How about by your desk?

This is the flag of the United States.

The flag is red, white, and blue.

It has 13 stripes. It has 50 stars.

Each of the stars stands for a state.

The flag stands for freedom.

Name: ______________________ Date: ____________

Directions: Listen to and read "The U.S. Flag." Answer the questions.

1. What is this text mostly about?
   - (A) the flag of the United States
   - (B) things you see at school
   - (C) clothes with stripes

2. What colors are on the U.S. flag?
   - (A) red, green, and orange
   - (B) red, white, and blue
   - (C) white, pink, and silver

3. How many stars are on the flag?
   - (A) 13
   - (B) 34
   - (C) 50

4. Which is another good title?
   - (A) Why We Stand
   - (B) The Desk and Sky
   - (C) All about the Flag

Name: ______________________________ Date: ____________

Directions: Listen to and read "The U.S. Flag" again. Draw a place where you might see the flag. Use the words to label your drawing.

flag	star	stripe	red	white	blue

Name: ______________________________ Date: ______________

Directions: Match the words to the pictures.

spot

spider

wasp

1. spider

2. spot

3. wasp

Directions: Circle the word for the picture. Write the word.

4.

spy spin

____

Name: ______________________________ Date: ____________

Directions: Match the words to the pictures.

swim

swan

sweet

1. swan

2. sweet

3. swim

Directions: Circle the word for the picture. Write the word.

4. 

sweep   swam

____

Name: ______________________________ Date: ____________

Directions: Listen to and read the sentences. Match the sentences to the pictures.

1. Stan wanted to swim.

2. Red flag means a risk.

3. They ate snacks.

Directions: Circle the word for the picture. Write the word.

4.

spider spot

Name: ______________________________ Date: ____________

Stay Safe

Stan and Mom went down for a swim. They spied a spot.

They asked if it was safe. The red flag means a risk. They did not swim.

Stan and Mom stayed safe on the sand. They ate snacks.

Name: ______________________ Date: ____________

Directions: Listen to and read "Stay Safe." Answer the questions.

1. What do Stan and Mom want to do?

(A) take a walk

(B) spy fish

(C) swim at the beach

2. What do they ask?

(A) if it is safe to swim

(B) for a snack

(C) about the fish

3. What does the flag mean?

(A) It is a special day.

(B) The sky is clear.

(C) There is a risk.

4. What do Stan and Mom do instead of swim?

(A) have snacks

(B) skip in the sand

(C) speed home

Name: ______________________ Date: ____________

Directions: Listen to and read "Stay Safe" again. What is one thing you want to do at the beach? Draw and label a picture.

Name: ______________________ Date: __________

Directions: Match the words to the pictures.

truck

dirt

tree

1. tree

2. truck

3. dirt

Directions: Circle the word for the picture. Write the word.

4. 

cart heart

____

Name: ______________________ Date: ____________

Directions: Match the words to the pictures.

chirp

grass

sharp

1. chirp

2. sharp

3. grass

Directions: Circle the word for the picture. Write the word.

4. 

graze grin

____

Name: ______________________ Date: __________

Directions: Listen to and read the sentences. Match the sentences to the pictures.

1. Ride in a tractor.

2. Visit the greenhouse.

3. See cows graze on grass.

Directions: Circle the word for the picture. Write the word.

4.

trip tree

____

Name: ______________________ Date: ____________

Come Tour the Farm

Join us at Fran's Farm and have some fun!

Dig in the dirt with the worms. Plant some seeds.

Ride a tractor or a truck.

See the greenhouse. Spy the big fern leaves inside.

See the cows graze on grass.

Listen to the birds chirp.

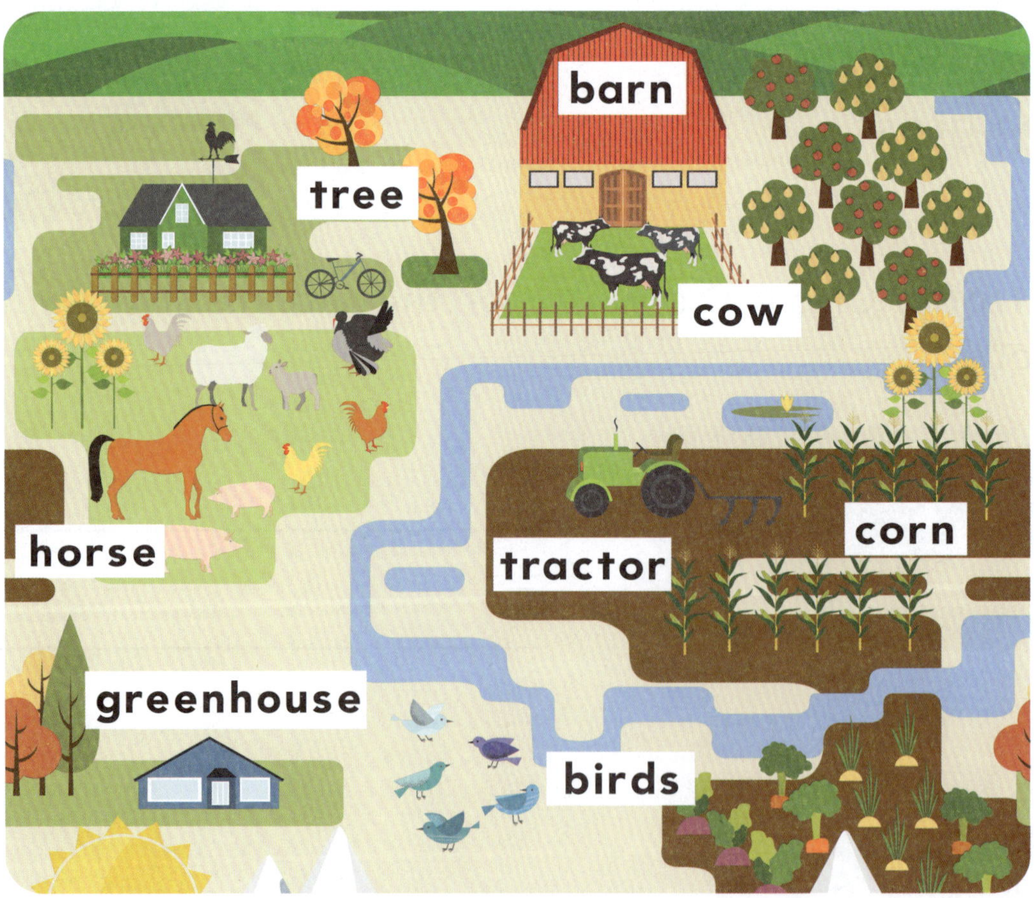

Name: ______________________________ Date: ____________

Directions: Listen to and read "Come Tour the Farm." Answer the questions.

1. What does *fern* mean?
   - (A) a frog
   - (B) a type of plant
   - (C) a truck

2. Which word helps you know the meaning of *fern*?
   - (A) leaves
   - (B) see
   - (C) big

3. What does *chirp* mean?
   - (A) sit on a tree
   - (B) make a small sound
   - (C) live in a barn

4. What word helps you know the meaning of *chirp*?
   - (A) grass
   - (B) farm
   - (C) listen

Name: ______________________ Date: ____________

Directions: Listen to and read "Come Tour the Farm" again. Draw one thing you can do if you visit the farm. Label your picture.

Name: ______________________ Date: ____________

Directions: Match the words to the pictures.

worm

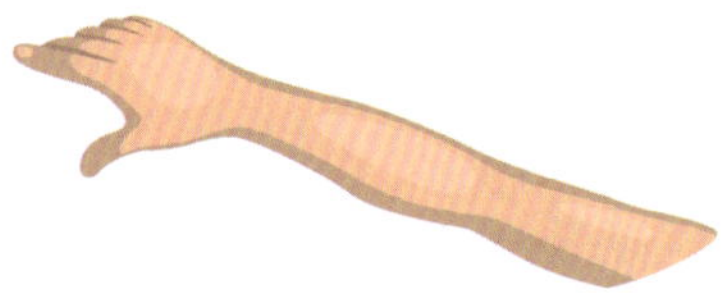

arm

warm

1. arm

2. warm

3. worm

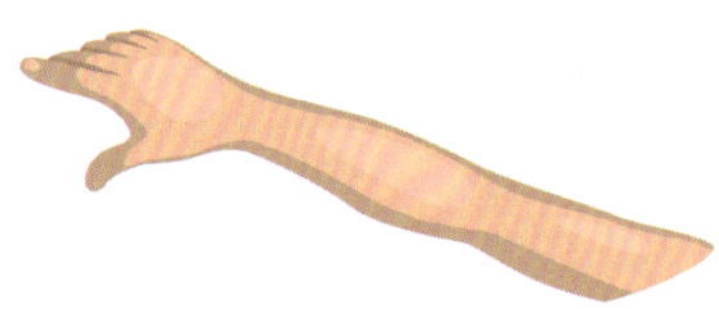

Directions: Circle the word for the picture. Write the word.

4.

farm harm

____

Name: ______________________ Date: ____________

Directions: Match the words to the pictures.

crow

crib

cry

1. cry

2. crow

3. crib

Directions: Circle the word for the picture. Write the word.

4. 

crash   crop

____

Name: ______________________________ Date: ____________

Directions: Listen to and read the phrases. Match the phrases to the pictures.

1. crow on the corn

2. bird chirps

3. grass in the cart

Directions: Circle the word for the picture. Write the word.

4.

worm   germ

____

Name: ______________________ Date: ____________

Fun on the Farm

Turk meets his friend Trish. They visit a farm. They see black crows near the grass. They hear birds chirp and cows moo. They feel the corn in the cart. They eat the fruit. They see the brown dirt.

What is that in the dirt? They dig and dig to get a worm. But they do not catch it.

Name: ______________________________ Date: ____________

Directions: Listen to and read "Fun on the Farm." Answer the questions.

1. What does *catch* mean in the story?
   - (A) get
   - (B) chirp
   - (C) hurt

2. Why do the kids dig in the dirt?
   - (A) to plant seeds
   - (B) to catch a worm
   - (C) to look for frogs

3. What do the kids feel?
   - (A) the birds
   - (B) the cows
   - (C) the corn in the cart

4. Which is another good title?
   - (A) Crows Play in the Dirt
   - (B) A Visit to the Farm
   - (C) Pigs in the Pen

Name: ______________________________ Date: ____________

Directions: Listen to and read "Fun on the Farm" again. What might happen next? Draw a picture.

They dig and dig to get the worm.
But they do not catch it.

Name: ______________________________ Date: ____________

Directions: Match the words to the pictures.

		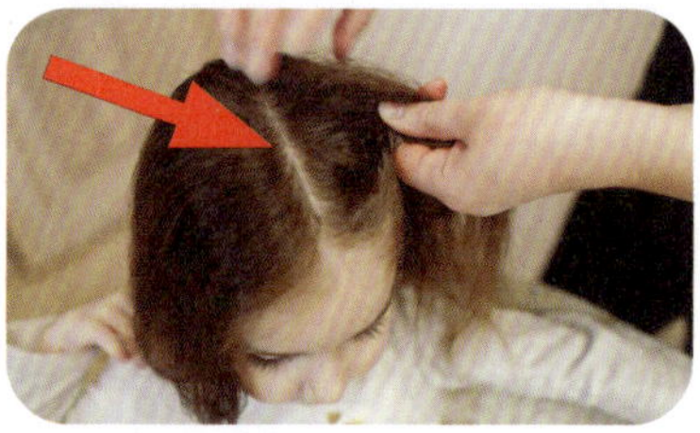
help	gulp	scalp

1. scalp 

2. help 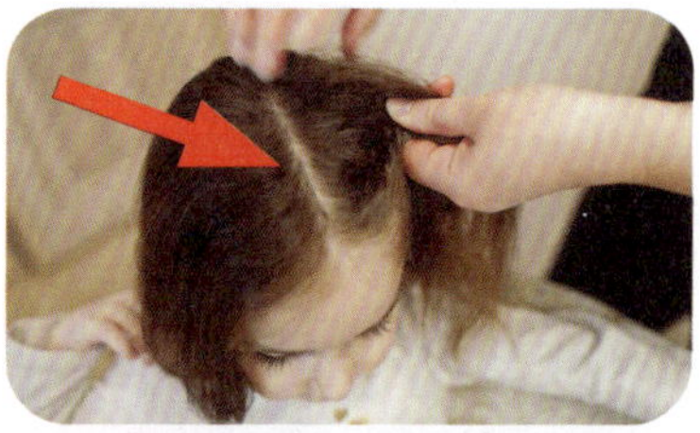

3. gulp 

Directions: Circle the word for the picture. Write the word.

4. 

yelp   kelp

____

Name: ______________________ Date: ____________

Directions: Match the words to the pictures.

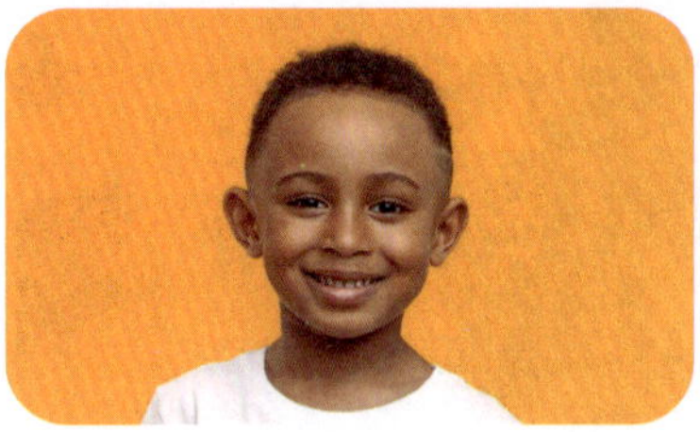

glad

glow

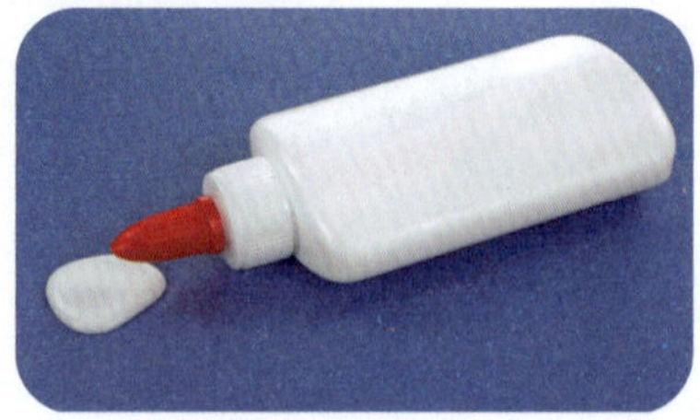

glue

1. glad

2. glow

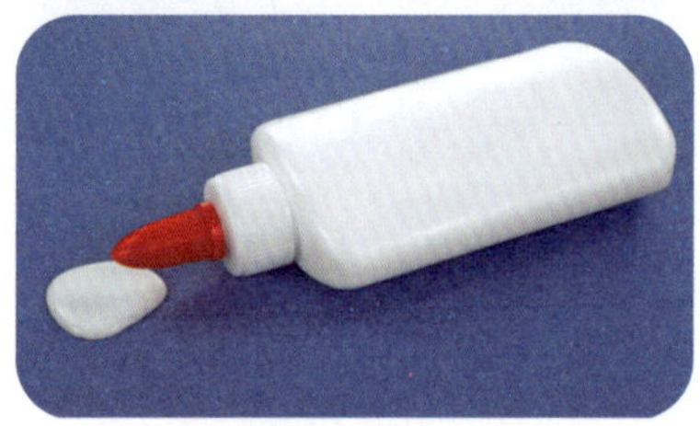

3. glue

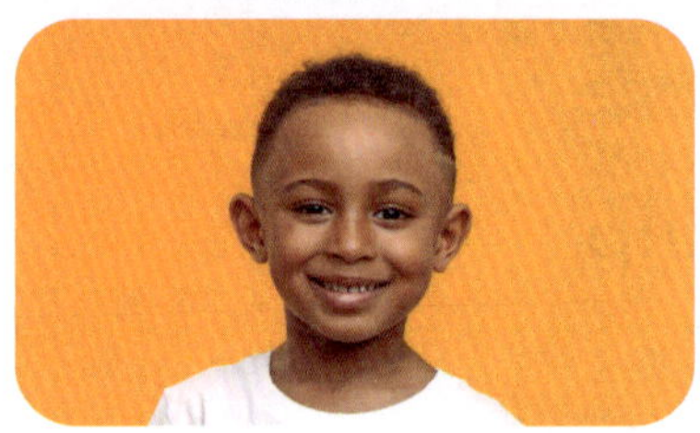

Directions: Circle the word for the picture. Write the word.

4. 

globe gloom

____

Name: ______________________________ Date: ____________

Directions: Listen to and read the phrases. Match the phrases to the pictures.

1. cross the street

2. helps you glue

3. books on a shelf

Directions: Circle the words that begin with *cl*. Write the words.

4. Help keep the class clean.

Name: ______________________________ Date: _____________

School Helpers

They read to you. They help you glue. They keep the class calm.

teachers

They help you get books from the shelf.

librarians

They are glad to see you.
They are happy to talk to you.

principals

They help you cross the street.

crossing guards

They keep the floors clean.
They keep the rooms clean.

janitors

They help you get to school.
They help you get back home.

bus drivers

Name: ______________________________ Date: ____________

Directions: Listen to and read "School Helpers." Answer the questions.

1. Who might drive you to school and back home?

   Ⓐ a principal
   Ⓑ a bus driver
   Ⓒ a librarian

2. Who helps you cross the street?

   Ⓐ a cook
   Ⓑ a janitor
   Ⓒ a crossing guard

3. In the text, who is glad to see you?

   Ⓐ a janitor
   Ⓑ a bus driver
   Ⓒ the principal

4. Which is another good title?

   Ⓐ Friends
   Ⓑ Adults at School
   Ⓒ My Classroom

Name: ______________________ Date: ____________

Directions: Listen to and read "School Helpers" again. Choose a different helper at school. Draw and write about them.

Name: ______________________ Date: __________

Directions: Match the words to the pictures.

talk

walk

milk

1. milk

2. talk

3. walk

Directions: Circle the word for the picture. Write the word.

4.

silk yolk

____

Name: ______________________ Date: ______________

Directions: Match the words to the pictures.

bloom

blade

black

1. blade 

2. black 

3. bloom 

Directions: Circle the word for the picture. Write the word.

4.

blob blink

____

Name: ______________________________ Date: ____________

Directions: Listen to and read the sentences. Match the sentences to the pictures.

1. They start to play.

2. Dad gives them milk.

3. Teacher welcomes them to class.

Directions: Circle the word for the picture. Write the word.

4.

calf   half

____

Name: ______________________ Date: ____________

Getting to School

Oh no! Clark and Flora are not ready for school. They woke up and started to play.

Everyone needs to help get them there on time.

Mom helps each child get dressed. Granddad helps put on their black shoes.

Dad gives them milk. Brother cleans their faces.

Aunty holds the door. Cousin holds their hands.

Teacher welcomes them to class.

Name: ______________________ Date: ____________

Directions: Listen to and read "Getting to School." Answer the questions.

1. Who are Clark and Flora?
   - (A) Grandma and Grandpa
   - (B) Mom and Dad
   - (C) kids who are late to school

2. How does Aunty help?
   - (A) She wakes them up.
   - (B) She holds the door.
   - (C) She talks to them.

3. Why are the kids running late?
   - (A) They start to play.
   - (B) They wake up late.
   - (C) They have milk.

4. Which is another good title?
   - (A) Drinking Milk
   - (B) Getting Dressed
   - (C) Hurry Up!

Name: ______________________ Date: ____________

Directions: Listen to and read "Getting to School" again. Have you ever been late? Draw and write about it.

Name: ______________________________ Date: ____________

Directions: Match the words to the pictures.

car	jar	star

1. jar

2. star

3. car

Directions: Circle the word for the picture. Write the word.

4. 

scar bar

____

Name: ______________________________ Date: ____________

Directions: Match the words to the pictures.

warm

dark

yard

1. dark

2. yard

3. warm

Directions: Circle the word for the picture. Write the word.

4. 

part garden

____

Name: ______________________________ Date: ____________

Directions: Listen to and read the phrases. Match the phrases to the pictures.

1. a dark night

2. near a garden

3. a clear jar

Directions: Circle the *ar* word. Write the word.

4. They may land on
your arm.

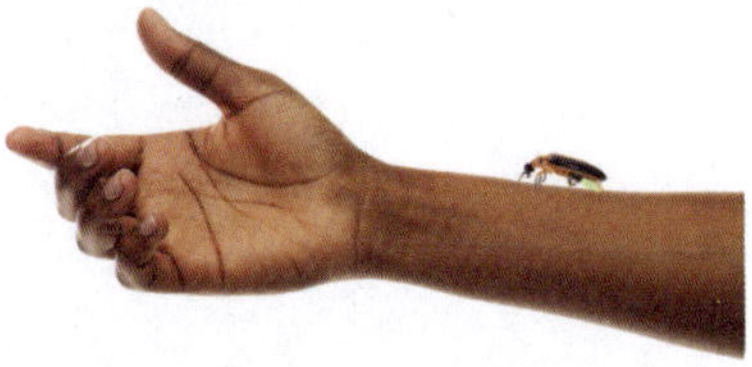

____

Name: ______________________ Date: __________

How to Catch Fireflies

Go outside with a clear jar on a warm night.

Get a flashlight. Cover it with blue paper. Use it to look in the grass by a garden.

Watch their light as they dart. Start to flash your light like them. They may find you and land on your arm.

Use your hand to cup them. Put them in the jar. Now you have a jar of stars!

Note: Be sure to put holes in the lid of the jar if you follow these directions.

Name: ______________________________ Date: ____________

Directions: Listen to and read "How to Catch Fireflies." Answer the questions.

1. What is this text teaching you?
   - (A) how to sleep on warm nights
   - (B) the best way to catch fireflies
   - (C) things you can do with a jar

2. What should you do with your flashlight?
   - (A) Keep it turned off.
   - (B) Wave it around.
   - (C) Cover it with blue paper.

3. What should you do after you cup a firefly in your hand?
   - (A) Put it in a jar.
   - (B) Shine a light on it.
   - (C) Take it to a barn.

4. Which is another good title?
   - (A) Get a Flashlight
   - (B) Catching Fireflies
   - (C) Fun in the Sun

Name: ______________________ Date: ____________

Directions: Listen to and read "How to Catch Fireflies" again. Draw how you would catch fireflies. Write words to go with your picture.

Name: ______________________ Date: __________

Directions: Match the words to the pictures.

far

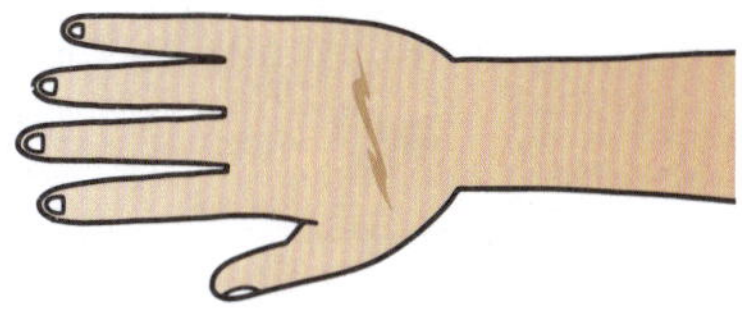
scar

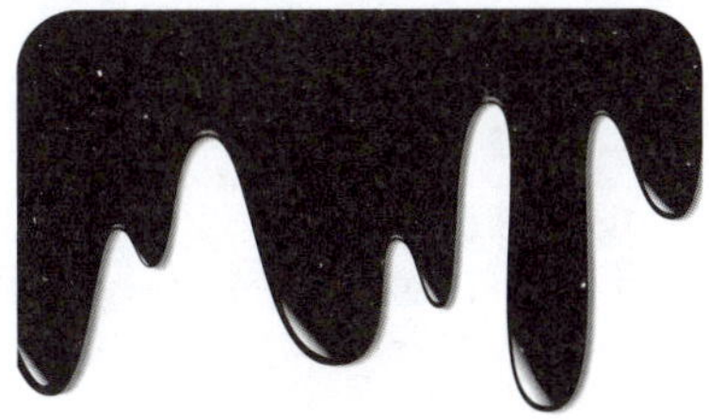
tar

1. far

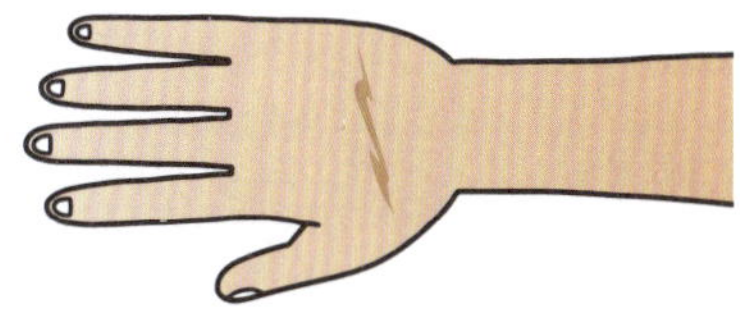

2. scar

3. tar

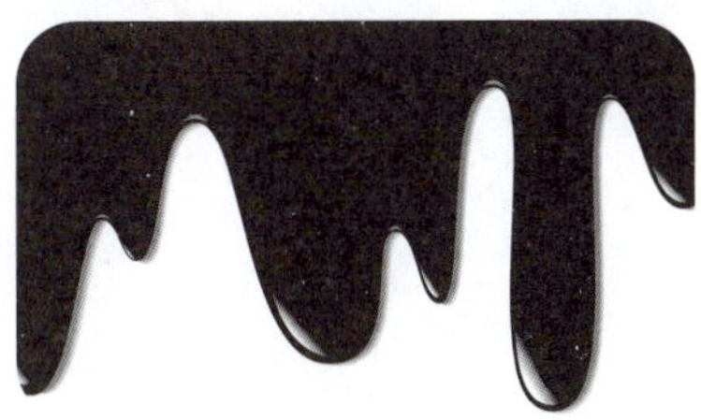

Directions: Circle the word for the picture. Write the word.

4. 

start art

____

Name: ______________________________ Date: ____________

Directions: Match the words to the pictures.

party

start

warm

1. party

2. start

3. warm

Directions: Circle the word for the picture. Write the word.

4.

barn shark

____

Name: ______________________________ Date: ______________

Directions: Listen to and read the sentences. Match the sentences to the pictures.

1. Omar and Char rode far.

2. They look in the garden.

3. They look up at the stars.

Directions: Circle the *ar* word. Write the word.

4. The shark is in the water.

____

Name: ______________________________ Date: ____________

Omar and Char Go Camping

Omar and Char go far to camp. The sky is dark. It is hard to stay awake.

They look up at the stars. They start to sing.

They look in the garden. They see fireflies. It looks like they are having a party!

Name: ______________________________ Date: ____________

Directions: Listen to and read "Omar and Char Go Camping." Answer the questions.

1. Where are Omar and Char going?
   - (A) to art camp
   - (B) camping
   - (C) to school

2. What do they do to stay awake?
   - (A) look at the stars and sing
   - (B) play games
   - (C) wear a scarf

3. What do they see in the garden?
   - (A) a horse and cart
   - (B) a lot of fireflies
   - (C) a barn

4. The fireflies look like they are ________.
   - (A) starting to fly
   - (B) making a mark
   - (C) having a party

Name: ______________________________ Date: ____________

Directions: Listen to and read "Omar and Char Go Camping" again. Draw what you think will happen next. Write words to go with your picture.

Name: ______________________ Date: __________

Directions: Match the words to the pictures.

fort

form

storm

1. form

2. storm

3. fort

Directions: Circle the word for the picture. Write the word.

4.

sort horn

____

Name: ______________________________ Date: ____________

Directions: Match the words to the pictures.

thorn

morning

short

1. morning

2. thorn

3. short

Directions: Circle the word for the picture. Write the word.

4.

cord cork

____

Name: ______________________________ Date: ____________

Directions: Listen to and read the sentences. Match the sentences to the pictures.

1. Clouds will form.

2. A jacket should be worn.

3. Look for colorful rainbows in the morning.

Directions: Circle the *or* words. Write the words.

4. There will be a short storm.

____

____

Name: ____________________ Date: ____________

Weather Report

Tuesday

Clouds will form. Watch for a big storm. A jacket should be worn.

Wednesday

It will be cloudy today. The storm will bring a lot of rain.

Thursday

The storm will be gone. But there will be short times of rain. The sun will come out. Look for colorful rainbows in the morning.

Name: ______________________________ Date: ____________

Directions: Listen to and read "Weather Report." Answer the questions.

1. In the text, what does *worn* mean?

- (A) very tired
- (B) old
- (C) put on your body

2. *Colorful* means ________.

- (A) lots of colors
- (B) clouds and rain
- (C) sun

3. In the text, what will the clouds do?

- (A) form
- (B) be short
- (C) hide

4. Why did the author write this text?

- (A) to tell a story
- (B) to draw a picture
- (C) to tell the weather

Name: ______________________________ Date: ____________

Directions: Listen to and read "Weather Report" again. Draw and label what you would wear on Wednesday. Use the text to help you decide.

Name: ______________________ Date: ____________

Directions: Match the words to the pictures.

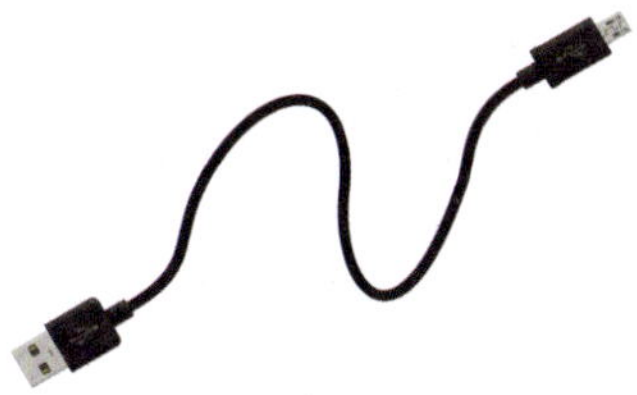

cord

torch

sport

1. torch
2. cord
3. sport

Directions: Circle the word for the picture. Write the word.

4.

door cork

____

Name: ______________________ Date: ____________

Directions: Match the words to the pictures.

porch

corn

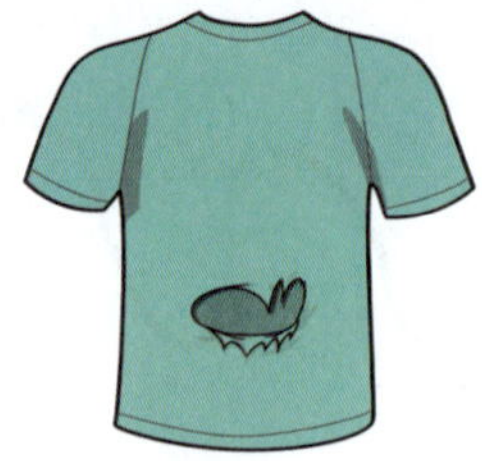

torn

1. torn

2. porch

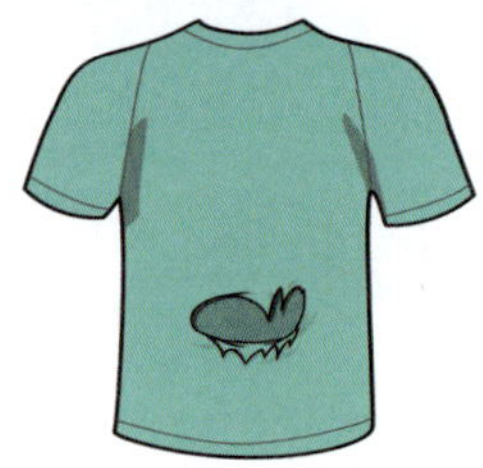

3. corn

Directions: Circle the word for the picture. Write the word.

4.

sort sword

____

Name: ______________________ Date: __________

Directions: Listen to and read the sentences. Match the sentences to the pictures.

1. Cora woke up in the morning.

2. She got ready for her sport.

3. She heard a storm and ran to her front porch.

Directions: Circle the *or* word. Write the word.

4. She ran out the door to play in the rain.

____

Name: ______________________________ Date: ____________

Rainy Morning

Cora wakes up. She gets ready. She is going to play her sport.

She hears a storm. She runs to her front porch. She looks out to the corner. Grey clouds have formed. It is rainy today.

She gets her boots and hat. She runs out the door to play in the rain.

Name: ______________________________ Date: ____________

Directions: Listen to and read "Rainy Morning." Answer the questions.

1. *Rainy* means ________.
   - (A) waking up early
   - (B) the clouds are short
   - (C) there is rain

2. What is an example of a *sport*?
   - (A) going to school
   - (B) soccer
   - (C) sleeping

3. What does Cora see when she looks at the corner?
   - (A) clouds have formed
   - (B) kids playing sports
   - (C) colorful hats and boots

4. Which is another good title?
   - (A) Cora's Cat
   - (B) No Sport for Cora
   - (C) A Hot Day

Name: ______________________________ Date: ____________

Directions: Listen to and read "Rainy Morning" again. Draw what you think will happen next. Write words to go with your picture.

Name: ______________________ Date: ____________

Directions: Match the words to the pictures.

twirl

bird

first

1. bird

2. first

3. twirl

Directions: Circle the word for the picture. Write the word.

4.

skirt   shirt

____

Name: ______________________________ Date: ____________

Directions: Match the words to the pictures.

shirt

circle

whirl

1. whirl

2. shirt

3. circle

Directions: Circle the word for the picture. Write the word.

4.

birth dirty

____

Name: ______________________________ Date: ____________

Directions: Listen to and read the sentences. Match the sentences to the pictures.

1. They love to twirl in a circle.

2. Canaries like to chirp.

3. Lovebirds like to sit on your shirt.

Directions: Circle the *ir* word. Write the word.

4. Finches make great first pets.

____

Name: ______________________________ Date: ____________

The Best Pet Birds

Parakeets are friendly birds. They love their owners. They love to twirl in a circle.

parakeet

Canaries like to chirp and twirl. They are easy to care for. They like to be alone.

canary

Finches are great first pets. They are small. They love to chirp and sing. They won't fly in the air.

finch

Lovebirds are fun. They like to sit on your shirt. Get two. They are best in pairs.

lovebirds

Name: ______________________ Date: __________

Directions: Listen to and read "The Best Pet Birds." Answer the questions.

1. Which two kinds of birds like to chirp?
   - (A) parakeets and canaries
   - (B) canaries and lovebirds
   - (C) canaries and finches

2. The word *pair* means ________.
   - (A) cage
   - (B) two
   - (C) fun

3. Canaries and parakeets both like to ________.
   - (A) twirl
   - (B) dance
   - (C) fly away

4. Which birds does the text say make great first pets?
   - (A) finches
   - (B) lovebirds
   - (C) parakeets

Name: ______________________________ Date: ____________

Directions: Listen to and read "The Best Pet Birds" again. Which bird would you choose for a pet? Draw and write your answer.

Name: ______________________ Date: ____________

Directions: Match the words to the pictures.

stir

girl

third

1. third

2. girl

3. stir

Directions: Circle the word for the picture. Write the word.

4.

circle circus

____

Name: ____________________ Date: __________

Directions: Match the words to the pictures.

dirt

skirt

thirst

1. skirt

2. dirt

3. thirst

Directions: Circle the word for the picture. Write the word.

4.

tired twirl

____

Name: ______________________________ Date: ____________

Directions: Listen to and read the sentences. Match the sentences to the pictures.

1. The daddy bird wakes first.

2. He starts to pull.

3. The brood begins to chirp.

Directions: Circle the *ir* word. Write the word.

4. He spots a squirmy worm.

____

Name: ______________________________ Date: ____________

Early Bird Gets the Worm

Irvin gets up first.

He scoots to the dirt. He starts to swirl.

He is hungry. He looks high and low. The dirt starts to stir! The bird spots a big worm. The worm squirms.

His beak starts to dig and swirl. He starts to pull.

He goes back to his nest. The brood begins to chirp and twirl.

Unit 13
WEEK 2
DAY
4

Name: ______________________ Date: __________

Directions: Listen to and read "Early Bird Gets the Worm." Answer the questions.

1. Who is Irvin?

   (A) the girl
   (B) the bird
   (C) the worm

2. Where does this story take place?

   (A) in a house
   (B) outside near a nest
   (C) at a school

3. What happens after the bird sees the worm?

   (A) The bird starts to dig.
   (B) He sings and chirps.
   (C) He flies away.

4. Which is another good title?

   (A) The Worm Gets Away
   (B) Irvin Feeds his Brood
   (C) The Bird Goes Inside

Name: ______________________ Date: ____________

Directions: Listen to and read "Early Bird Gets the Worm" again. Draw and label what you think will happen next.

Name: ______________________ Date: __________

Directions: Match the words to the pictures.

dinner

butter

fern

1. fern

2. dinner

3. butter

Directions: Circle the word for the picture. Write the word.

4. 

germ herd

____

Name: ______________________ Date: __________

Directions: Match the words to the pictures.

surf

burger

yogurt

1. burger

2. surf

3. yogurt

Directions: Circle the word for the picture. Write the word.

4.

turn burn

Name: ______________________ Date: ____________

Directions: Listen to and read the phrases. Match the phrases to the pictures.

1. pizza with peppers

2. butter noodles

3. circle crackers with cheese

Directions: Circle the *er* word. Write the word.

4. I'll take the big, big burger.

____

Name: ______________________ Date: ____________

The Perch

We are happy to serve you!

Dinner Menu

surf and turf

butter noodles

herb turkey

pizza with peppers

burger and tater tots

chicken tenders

circle crackers with cheese

corn dogs

Save room for dessert!
We have yogurt pie.

Our food is never burnt.

Name: ______________________ Date: ___________

Directions: Listen to and read "The Perch." Answer the questions.

1. What type of menu is this?
   - (A) a breakfast menu
   - (B) a dessert menu
   - (C) a dinner menu

2. What shape are the crackers with cheese?
   - (A) circle
   - (B) triangle
   - (C) square

3. What is on the pizza?
   - (A) peppers
   - (B) butter
   - (C) herbs

4. The food at The Perch is ________.
   - (A) always hot
   - (B) never burnt
   - (C) sometimes cold

Name: ______________________ Date: ____________

Directions: Listen to and read "The Perch" again. Draw and label what you would order.

Name: ______________________________ Date: ____________

Directions: Match the words to the pictures.

herb	germ	her

1. germ 

2. her 

3. herb 

Directions: Circle the word for the picture. Write the word.

4. 

alert   over

____

Name: ______________________ Date: ____________

Directions: Match the words to the pictures.

furry

surf

curl

1. surf

2. furry

3. curl

Directions: Circle the word for the picture. Write the word.

4.

hurt   purr

____

Name: ______________________ Date: __________

Directions: Listen to and read the sentences. Match the sentences to the pictures.

1. Harper sat down for dinner.

2. The dog barked.

3. The dog walked in a circle.

Directions: Circle the *er* word. Write the word.

4. Murry did not want his dinner.

____

Name: ______________________________ Date: ____________

Dinner Time

Harper sat down to eat dinner. She ate surf and turf. She sat next to her furry dog, Murry. He did not want to eat his dinner.

He wanted the surf and turf. He did not want his food. He barked and barked.

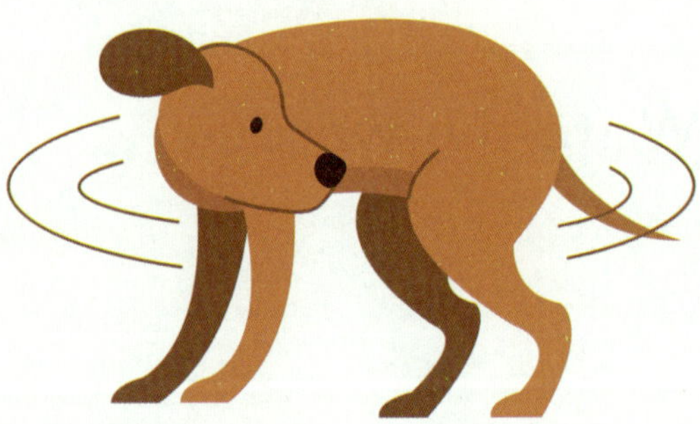

He walked in a circle. Harper tried to eat. It was too loud.

Harper took him to her porch. Murry was not happy.

Name: ______________________________ Date: ____________

Directions: Listen to and read "Dinner Time." Answer the questions.

1. Where does Harper try to eat her dinner?
   - (A) at the table
   - (B) on the floor
   - (C) on the porch

2. What does Murry want?
   - (A) his food
   - (B) Harper's dinner
   - (C) a bowl of mush

3. What does Murry do to bother Harper?
   - (A) He sits too close.
   - (B) He falls asleep.
   - (C) He barks and barks.

4. Which is another good title?
   - (A) Picky Murry
   - (B) Murry and Harper Eat Dinner
   - (C) Murry Loves Mush

Name: ____________________ Date: __________

Directions: Listen to and read "Dinner Time" again. Draw and write about what you think will happen next.

Name: ______________________ Date: __________

Directions: Match the words to the pictures.

shell

ship

shade

1. shell
2. shade
3. ship

Directions: Circle the word for the picture. Write the word.

4. 

show sharp

____

Name: ______________________ Date: ____________

Directions: Match the words to the pictures.

wish

brush

cash

1. cash

2. wish

3. brush

Directions: Circle the word for the picture. Write the word.

4. 

trash flush

____

Name: ______________________________ Date: ____________

Directions: Listen to and read the phrases. Match the phrases to the pictures.

1. snail in a shell

2. the shield protects

3. shape of a circle

Directions: Circle the *sh* word. Write the word.

4. They can be found on shrubs.

____

Name: ____________________ Date: ____________

Animals with Shells

Snails

They can go in their shells. This gives them shelter. They can hide from danger.

King Crabs

They are big and good to eat. People in ships go fish for them. They wish for them to be in their nets.

Turtles

Heavy shells and small legs mean they do not go fast. Their shells are like shields. They give them shade.

Sea Urchins

They live in the water. They have a round shape. Sharp spikes are on their shells. They look like a brush.

Beetles

They can be found on shrubs. Their shells help them push dirt.

Name: ______________________________ Date: ____________

Directions: Listen to and read "Animals with Shells." Answer the questions.

1. Which two animals with shells live in the water?
   - (A) turtle and snail
   - (B) king crab and sea urchin
   - (C) snail and beetle

2. In the text, which two animals use their shells for protection?
   - (A) turtle and snail
   - (B) beetle and sea urchin
   - (C) crab and turtle

3. Which animal has small legs?
   - (A) crab
   - (B) turtle
   - (C) snail

4. Which animal does the text say is big?
   - (A) beetle
   - (B) snail
   - (C) king crab

Name: ______________________ Date: ____________

Directions: Listen to and read "Animals with Shells" again. Choose one of the animals from the text. Draw and write about it.

Name: ______________________ Date: __________

Directions: Match the words to the pictures.

shoe

ship

sheep

1. ship

2. sheep

3. shoe

Directions: Circle the word for the picture. Write the word.

4.

short shelf

____

Name: ______________________ Date: ____________

Directions: Match the words to the pictures.

push

wash

flash

1. flash

2. push

3. wash

Directions: Circle the word for the picture. Write the word.

4.

lash crash

____

Name: ______________________ Date: ____________

Directions: Listen to and read the sentences. Match the sentences to the pictures.

1. She washed her shell.

2. She put on her shoes.

3. Dash took a short walk.

Directions: Circle the *sh* word. Write the word.

4. The crab is on the shore.

____

Name: ______________________ Date: __________

Fast Dash

Dash the turtle was not slow. But she also was not fast. She had a wish. She wanted to run past the crab at the shore. The crab was very fast.

She thought, *This is not such a big wish. All I need is a good coach.*

She washed her shell and put on her shoes.

Dash took a short walk to the sheep. She asked for help.

The sheep had Dash drill and drill and drill.

Dash got fast. She pushed past the crab. She won the race!

Name: ______________________________ Date: ____________

Directions: Listen to and read "Fast Dash." Answer the questions.

1. Who is the story mostly about?

- (A) the crab
- (B) the turtle
- (C) the sheep

2. Who helps coach and drill Dash?

- (A) the crab
- (B) the turtle
- (C) the sheep

3. What happens at the end of the story?

- (A) The turtle wins a race.
- (B) The turtle asks the sheep for help.
- (C) The turtle is sad.

4. What is Dash's wish?

- (A) to go to the shore
- (B) to lay in the shade
- (C) to win a race against the crab

Name: ______________________ Date: ____________

Directions: Listen to and read "Fast Dash" again. Draw and write what you think will happen next.

Name: ______________________________ Date: __________

Directions: Match the words to the pictures.

tooth

smooth

think

1. smooth

2. think

3. tooth

Directions: Circle the word for the picture. Write the word.

4.

thread think

____

Name: ______________________ Date: ____________

Directions: Match the words to the pictures.

whale

wheel

wheat

1. wheat

2. whale

3. wheel

Directions: Circle the word for the picture. Write the word.

4.

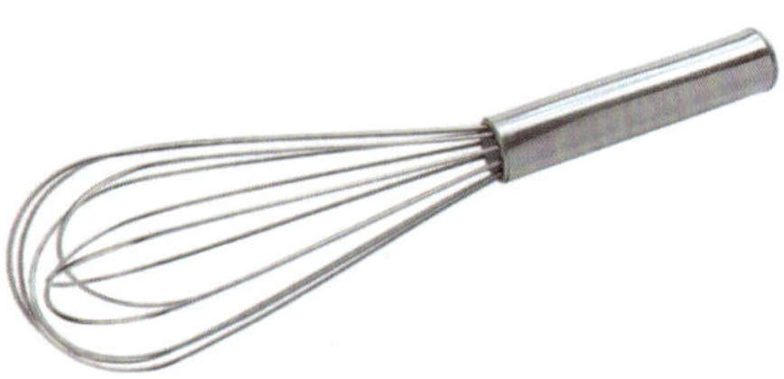

whisk whip

____

Name: ______________________ Date: __________

Directions: Listen to and read the sentences. Match the sentences to the pictures.

1. These whales have sharp teeth.

2. It helps the whale move in the water.

3. They have holes on top of their heads.

Directions: Circle the *wh* word. Write the word.

4. Whales live in the water.

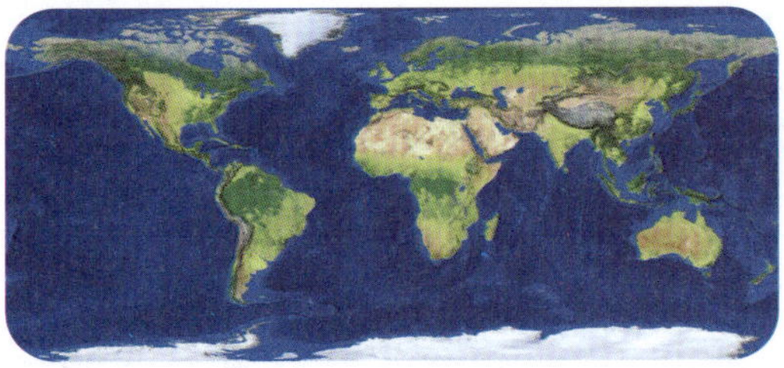

____

Name: ______________________ Date: ____________

Whales

Toothed

These whales have sharp teeth.

Baleen

This stuff is like a brush. It helps the whales trap food. They like to eat small fish and shrimp.

Where They Live

Whales live in the water. They live in oceans and seas.

More than Just Big

Each whale has a smooth body. Each one has a big tail. It helps the whale move in the water.

How They Breathe

They have holes on top of their heads. They use them to breathe. Air goes through. They blow and blow.

Name: ______________________ Date: __________

Directions: Listen to and read "Whales." Answer the questions.

1. What does *baleen* mean?
   - (A) sharp teeth
   - (B) brush to trap food
   - (C) how whales breathe

2. What are *seas*?
   - (A) a type of glasses
   - (B) how whales breathe
   - (C) water where whales live

3. What does a whale's big tail help it do?
   - (A) move through the water
   - (B) breathe
   - (C) eat shrimp and fish

4. How do baleen whales catch their food?
   - (A) They use their sharp teeth.
   - (B) They use their fins.
   - (C) They trap it in their mouths.

Name: ______________________ Date: ____________

Directions: Listen to and read "Whales" again. Draw a whale. Label the parts.

Name: ______________________ Date: ____________

Directions: Match the words to the pictures.

thick

broth

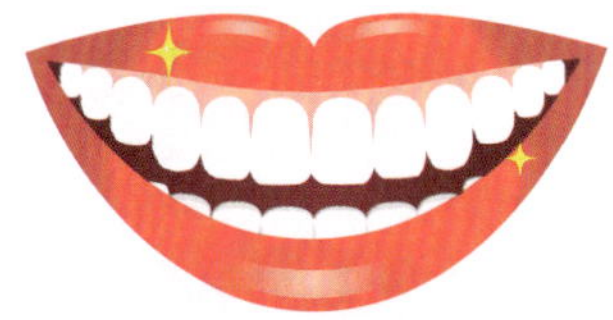
teeth

1. broth

2. thick

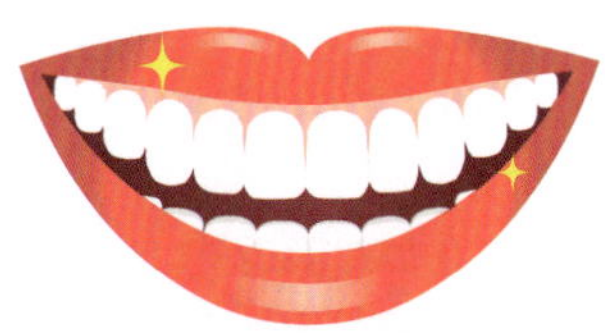

3. teeth

Directions: Circle the word for the picture. Write the word.

4.

cloth   moth

____

Name: ______________________ Date: ____________

Directions: Match the words to the pictures.

white

whiz

wham

1. wham

2. whiz

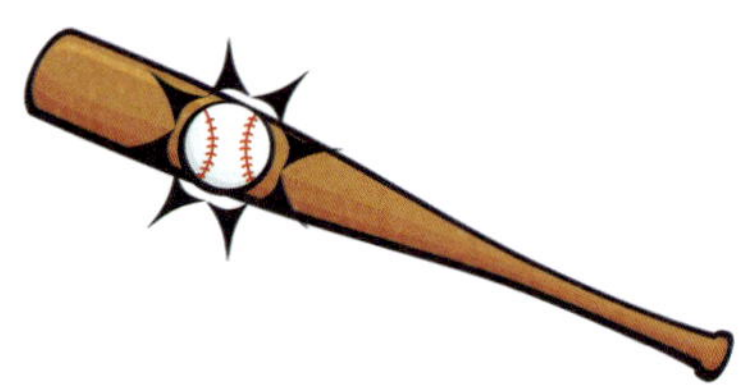

3. white

Directions: Circle the word for the picture. Write the word.

4.

whole why

____

Name: ______________________ Date: ____________

Directions: Listen to and read the sentences. Match the sentences to the pictures.

1. White whales fish in pods.

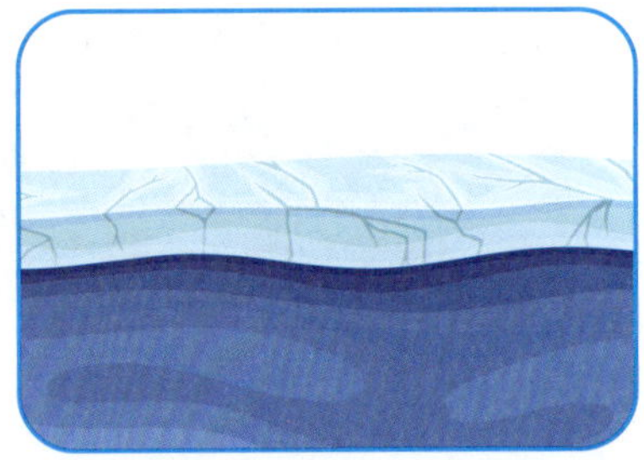

2. The ice started to get thick.

3. She held her breath and went deep.

Directions: Circle the *th* word. Write the word.

4. She heard both her mom and dad call.

____

Name: ______________________ Date: ____________

Whit Gets Lost

Whit the white whale went fishing with her pod.

She swam near the thick ice. She looked for shrimp. But she got lost.

The ice got thicker. She started to fret.

She heard both her mom and her dad click and call. She held her breath. She dove deep.

Whoops! She will not do that again.

Name: ______________________________ Date: ____________

Directions: Listen to and read "Whit Gets Lost." Answer the questions.

1. What does the word *thick* mean in the story?
   - (A) very close together
   - (B) not thin
   - (C) crowded

2. What helps you know the meaning of *pod*?
   - (A) the title
   - (B) the fish
   - (C) the picture

3. Which word helps you know the meaning of the word *dove*?
   - (A) deep
   - (B) breath
   - (C) click

4. Which is another good title?
   - (A) Whit Finds Shrimp
   - (B) At the Beach
   - (C) Whit Learns a Lesson

Name: ______________________ Date: __________

Directions: Listen to and read "Whit Gets Lost" again. Draw and write about what happens next.

Name: ______________________ Date: ____________

Directions: Match the words to the pictures.

peach

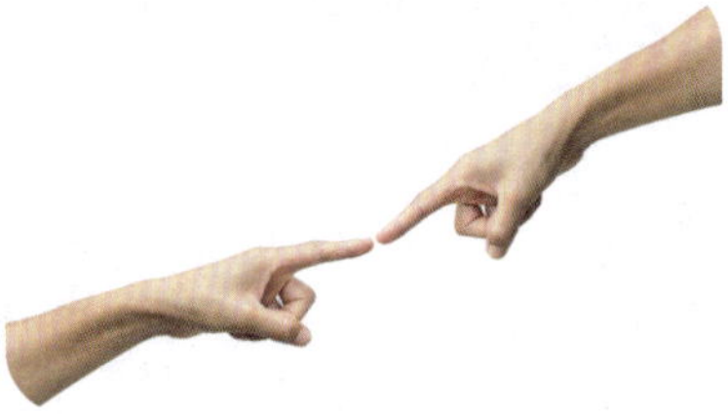
touch

rich

1. touch

2. rich

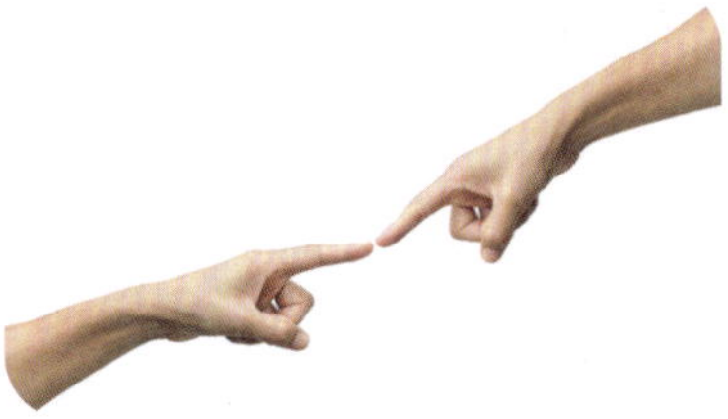

3. peach

Directions: Circle the word for the picture. Write the word.

4.

inch   branch

____

Name: ______________________ Date: ____________

Directions: Match the words to the pictures.

pick

pack

truck

1. pack

2. truck

3. pick

Directions: Circle the word for the picture. Write the word.

4. 

thick sticky

____

Name: ______________________ Date: __________

Directions: Listen to and read the sentences. Match the sentences to the pictures. Underline the *ch* in each word.

1. The peaches grow on the tree.

2. Many trees make an orchard.

3. This is one peach.

Directions: Circle the *ck* word in the sentence. Write the word.

4. The peach is sticky and juicy.

____

Name: ______________________ Date: __________

Peaches

Peaches grow on trees. They grow on the branches. Peach trees grow in orchards. These are big areas of trees.

They grow and grow. They need to be soft. Then, they are ready to be picked.

They are all picked. They are packed in a truck. They will go to the store.

The skin is fuzzy.

The flesh is sticky and juicy.

The pit is hard.

Name: ______________________________ Date: ____________

Directions: Listen to and read "Peaches." Answer the questions.

1. What is this text mostly about?
   - (A) soft fruit
   - (B) peaches
   - (C) apples

2. Peaches grow on _________.
   - (A) trees
   - (B) bushes
   - (C) trucks

3. How do you know when a peach is ready to be picked?
   - (A) It is round.
   - (B) It is orange.
   - (C) It is soft.

4. How do peaches get to the store?
   - (A) in trucks
   - (B) in carts
   - (C) on branches

Name: ______________________ Date: ____________

Directions: Listen to and read "Peaches" again. Draw how peaches get to the store. Write words to go with your picture.

Name: ______________________ Date: ____________

Directions: Match the words to the pictures.

chop

chart

teach

1. teach

2. chart

3. chop

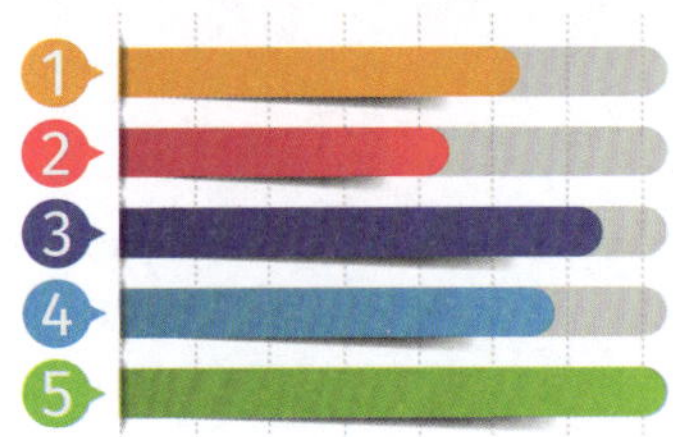

Directions: Circle the word for the picture. Write the word.

4.

catch chin

Name: ______________________ Date: ____________

Directions: Match the words to the pictures.

sack

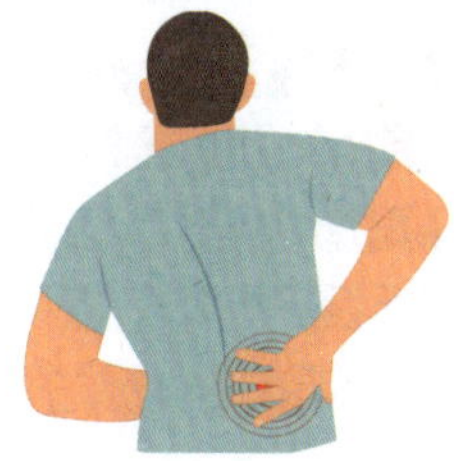
back

lick

1. lick

2. sack

3. back

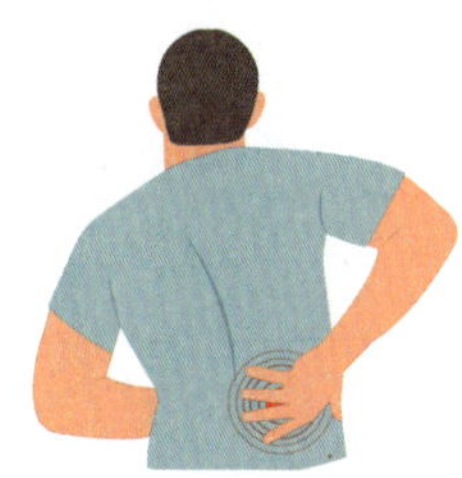

Directions: Circle the word for the picture. Write the word.

4.

neck shock

____

Name: ______________________ Date: ____________

Directions: Listen to and read the phrases. Match the phrases to the pictures.

1. a batch of peach pies

2. peaches in a sack

3. in the truck

Directions: Circle the picture that best matches the sentence.

4. He was shocked.

Name: ______________________ Date: ____________

First Place Pies

Charlie needs something for the fair. He talks to his dad. He asks him what to do. His dad can teach him how to make peach pie.

They get in the truck. They pick peaches. They put them in a sack.

They chop them up. They add sugar. But they do not add too much. They bake the pie

They were off the charts! Charlie wins first place.

Name: ______________________ Date: ____________

Directions: Listen to and read "First Place Pies." Answer the questions.

1. What happens at the beginning of the story?
   - (A) Charlie goes to school.
   - (B) Charlie cleans his room.
   - (C) Charlie talks to his dad.

2. What happens in the middle of the story?
   - (A) They go to the store.
   - (B) They pick peaches.
   - (C) They pick up Charlie's sister.

3. What do Charlie and his dad do when they get home?
   - (A) They make peach pie.
   - (B) They watch television.
   - (C) They go to bed.

4. What happens at the end of the story?
   - (A) Charlie wins first place.
   - (B) Charlie drops the pies.
   - (C) Charlie eats the pies.

Name: ______________________ Date: ____________

Directions: Listen to and read "First Place Pies" again. Draw and write what might happen next.

Name: ______________________ Date: __________

Directions: Match the words to the pictures.

wing

bring

sting

1. sting

2. wing

3. bring

Directions: Circle the word for the picture. Write the word.

4.

wring   string

____

Name: ______________________ Date: ____________

Directions: Match the words to the pictures.

eating

sing

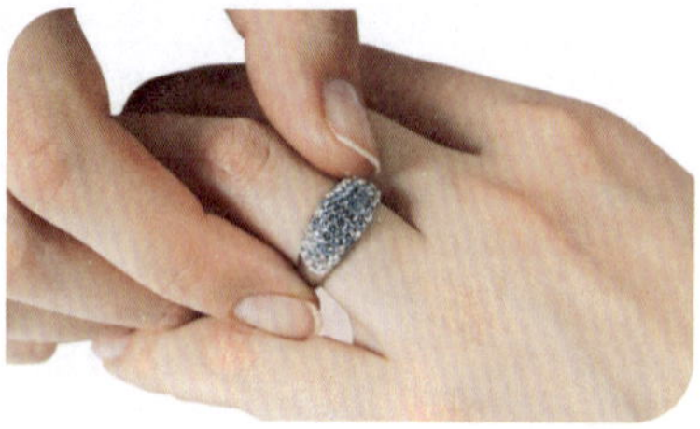

ring

1. ring

2. sing

3. eating

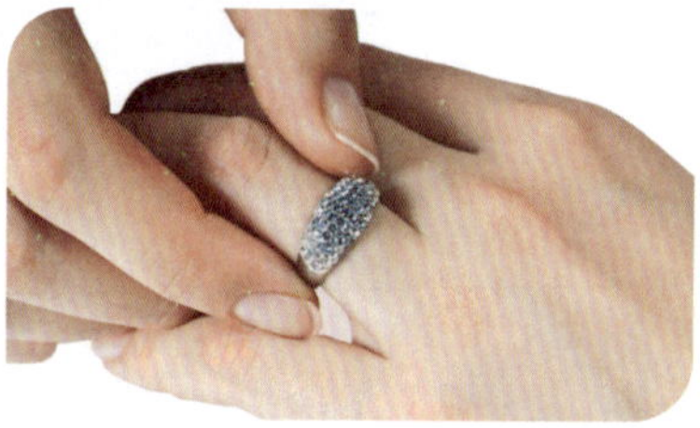

Directions: Circle the word for the picture. Write the word.

4. 

swing bingo

____

Name: ______________________ Date: ____________

Directions: Match the sentences to the pictures. Circle the word for  in each sentence.

1. The penguin is flapping its wings.

2. The penguin is gliding.

3. Two penguins are swimming.

Directions: Circle the *ing* word. Write the word.

4. They use their wings to fly in the sky.

____

Name: ______________________ Date: ____________

Wings

You can find wings on many things.

Birds, bees, and bats all fly.

They use their wings to climb in the sky.

But penguins can all be found using their wings on the ground.

They use them to waddle and slide.

They use them when swimming to help them glide.

Name: ______________________________ Date: ____________

Directions: Listen to and read "Wings." Answer the questions.

1. In the text, which animals use their wings to fly?
   - (A) birds and bees
   - (B) bees and penguins
   - (C) penguins and bats

2. How do penguins get around on the ground?
   - (A) waddling and sliding
   - (B) swimming and diving
   - (C) waddling and swimming

3. Most birds can _________, but penguins cannot.
   - (A) eat
   - (B) sleep
   - (C) fly

4. Which animals from the text are good swimmers?
   - (A) bees
   - (B) bats
   - (C) penguins

Name: ______________________ Date: __________

Directions: Listen to and read "Wings" again. Draw and write about your favorite animal with wings.

Name: ____________________ Date: __________

Directions: Match the words to the pictures.

king

string

biting

1. biting

2. king

3. string

Directions: Circle the word for the picture. Write the word.

4.

running licking

____

Name: ______________________ Date: ____________

Directions: Match the words to the pictures.

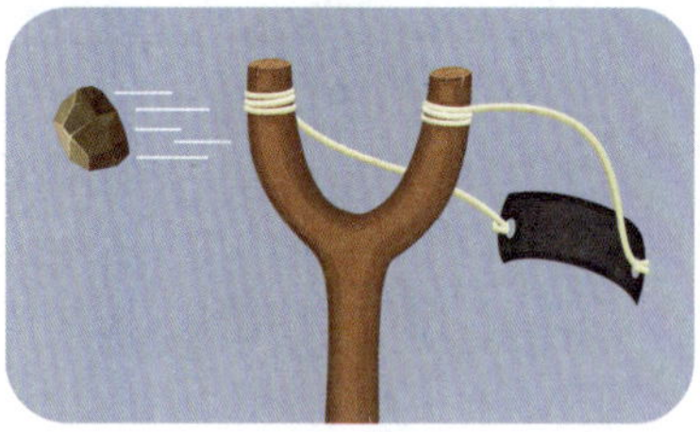
fling

gliding

spring

1. gliding

2. fling

3. spring

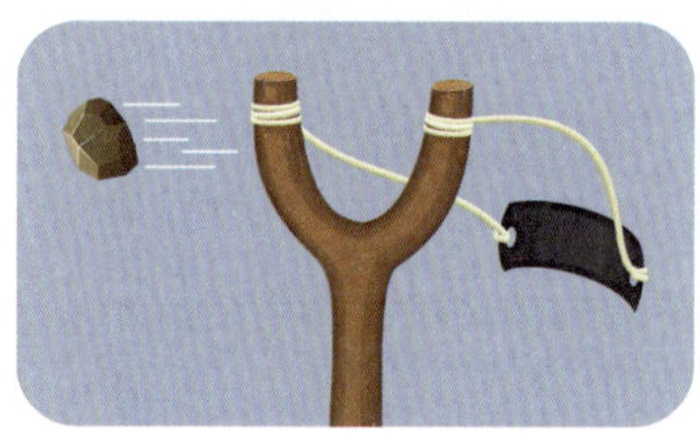

Directions: Circle the word for the picture. Write the word.

4.

swimming asking

____

Name: ______________________________ Date: ____________

Directions: Listen to and read the sentences. Match the sentences to the pictures.

1. Penguins are good at diving.

2. Two penguins went swimming.

3. The penguin was gliding on the ice.

Directions: Circle the *ing* word. Write the word.

4. The king penguin cannot fly.

____

Name: ______________________ Date: ____________

The King Who Could Not Fly

Ling was a king penguin. She did not think her wings worked right. She tried to cling. She tried to fling.

No matter what she did, her wings did not work. Then, she saw the others using their wings. She saw them swimming. She saw them flipping. She saw them gliding.

Ling tried these things. Then, she liked her wings!

Name: ______________________________ Date: ____________

Directions: Listen to and read "The King Who Could Not Fly." Answer the questions.

1. Who is the main character in the story?
   - (A) Ling
   - (B) a king
   - (C) a ring

2. What does Ling try and do with her wings?
   - (A) sing
   - (B) cling
   - (C) ding

3. What happens at the end of the story?
   - (A) The other penguins laugh at Ling.
   - (B) Ling likes her wings.
   - (C) Ling learns to fly.

4. Which is another good title?
   - (A) Ling Learns to Love Her Wings
   - (B) Penguins Shouldn't Have Wings
   - (C) The King Who Could Fly

Name: ______________________ Date: ____________

Directions: Listen to and read "The King Who Could Not Fly" again. Draw and write about what Ling might do next.

Standards Correlations

Shell Education is committed to producing educational materials that are research and standards based. To support this effort, this resource is correlated to the academic standards of all 50 states, the District of Columbia, the Department of Defense Dependent Schools, and the Canadian provinces. A correlation is also provided for key professional educational organizations.

To print a customized correlation report for your state, visit our website at **www.tcmpub.com/administrators/correlations** and follow the online directions. If you require assistance in printing correlation reports, please contact the Customer Service Department at 1-800-858-7339.

Standards Overview

The Every Student Succeeds Act (ESSA) mandates that all states adopt challenging academic standards that help students meet the goal of college and career readiness. While many states already adopted academic standards prior to ESSA, the act continues to hold states accountable for detailed and comprehensive standards. Standards are designed to focus instruction and guide adoption of curricula. They define the knowledge, skills, and content students should acquire at each level. Standards are also used to develop standardized tests to evaluate students' academic progress. State standards are used in the development of our resources, so educators can be assured they meet state academic requirements.

College and Career Readiness

Today's college and career readiness (CCR) standards offer guidelines for preparing K–12 students with the knowledge and skills that are necessary to succeed in postsecondary job training and education. CCR standards include the Common Core State Standards as well as other state-adopted standards such as the Texas Essential Knowledge and Skills. The standards found on page 228 describe the content presented throughout the lessons.

TESOL and WIDA Standards

English language development standards are integrated within each lesson to enable English learners to work toward proficiency in English while learning content–developing the skills and confidence in listening, speaking, reading, and writing. The standards found in the digital resources describe the language objectives presented throughout the lessons

Standards Correlations *(cont.)*

180 Days of Reading for Kindergarten Grade, 2nd Edition offers a full page of foundational skills and reading comprehension practice activities for each day of the school year.

Every unit provides questions and activities tied to a wide variety of language arts standards, providing students the opportunity for regular practice in reading comprehension, foundational skills, and writing. The focus of the first week in each unit is on nonfiction. The focus of the second week of each unit is on fiction.

Reading Comprehension
With prompting and support, ask and answer questions about key details in a text.
With prompting and support, identify characters, settings, and major events in a story.
Ask and answer questions about unknown words in a text.
Reading Foundational Skills
Distinguish between similarly spelled words by identifying the sounds of the letters that differ.
Demonstrate basic knowledge of letter-sound correspondences by producing the primary or most frequent sound for each consonant.
Associate the long and short sounds with the common spellings (graphemes) for the five major vowels.
Read common high-frequency words by sight.
Read emergent-reader texts with purpose and understanding.
Writing
Produce clear and coherent writing in which the development, organization, and style are appropriate to task, purpose, genre, and audience.
Use a combination of drawing, dictating, and writing to narrate a single event or several loosely linked events, tell about the events in the order in which they occurred, and provide a reaction to what happened.

Writing Rubric

Score students' Day 5 activities using the rubric below. Review and discuss the rubric with students.

Points	Criteria
4	• Uses drawing, dictating, and writing to express ideas. • Expresses multiple ideas on a topic. • Includes specific details, i.e., colors or size. • Spells with a letter to represent each sound, or in chunks of phonics patterns. • Demonstrates an intended purpose in writing.
3	• Uses drawing, dictating, and writing to express ideas. • Expresses at least one idea on a topic. • Spells with beginning and/or ending sounds.
2	• Uses only drawing and dictating to express ideas. • Attempts to express an idea on a topic. • Attempts to spell with beginning and/or ending sounds.
1	• Uses only drawing to express ideas. • Does not convey an idea that relates to the topic.
0	• Offers no writing, drawing, or dictating or does not respond to the assignment presented.

References Cited

Gough, Philip B., and William E. Tunmer. 1986. "Decoding, Reading, and Reading Disability." *Remedial and Special Education* 7 (1): 6–10.

Marzano, Robert. 2010. "When Practice Makes Perfect...Sense." *Educational Leadership* 68 (3): 81–83.

National Reading Panel. 2000. *Report of the National Reading Panel: Teaching Children to Read. Report of the Subgroups*. Washington, D.C.: U.S. Department of Health and Human Services, National Institutes of Health.

Scarborough, Hollis S. 2001. "Connecting Early Language and Literacy to Later Reading (Dis)abilities: Evidence, Theory, and Practice." In *Handbook of Early Literacy Research*, edited by Susan B. Neuman and David K. Dickinson, 97–110. New York: Guilford.

Soalt, Jennifer. 2005. "Bringing Together Fictional and Informational Texts to Improve Comprehension." *The Reading Teacher* 58 (7): 680–683.

Answer Key

Unit 1

Week 1

Day 1 (page 11)

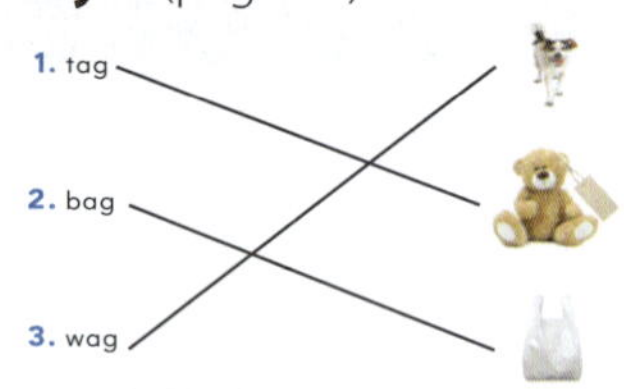

4. rag

Day 2 (page 12)

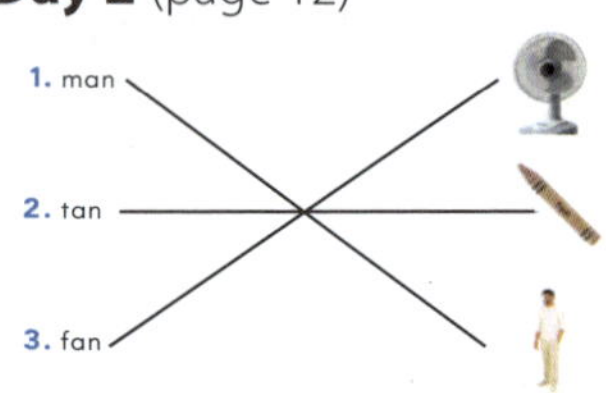

4. can

Day 3 (page 13)

1. bat, sat
2. bat, can
3. has
4. at

Day 4 (page 15)

1. B
2. A
3. A
4. C

Day 5 (page 16)

Answers should include a picture of a bat with the fang, wing, and ear circled.

Week 2

Day 1 (page 17)

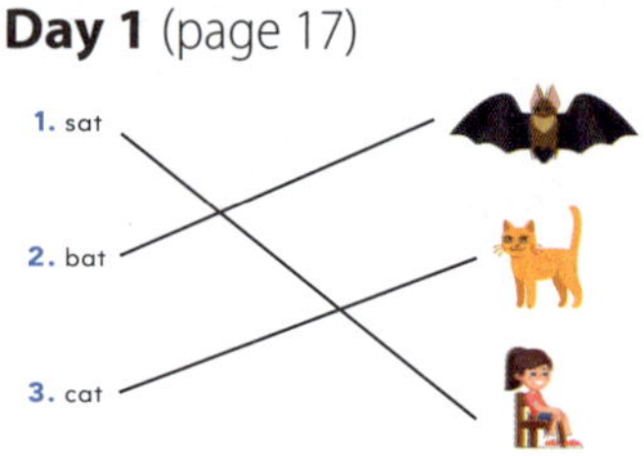

4. rat

Day 2 (page 18)

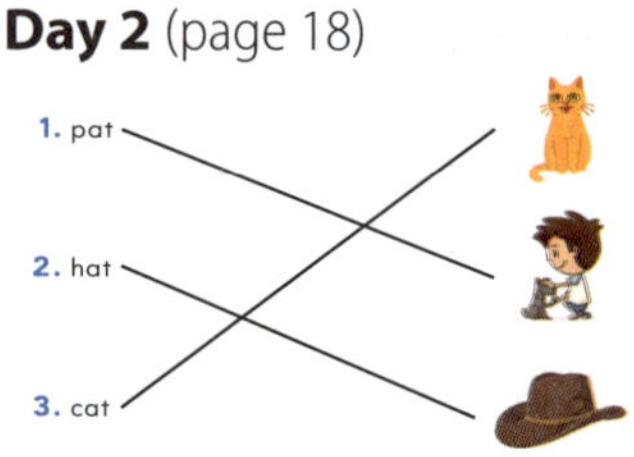

4. mat

Day 3 (page 19)

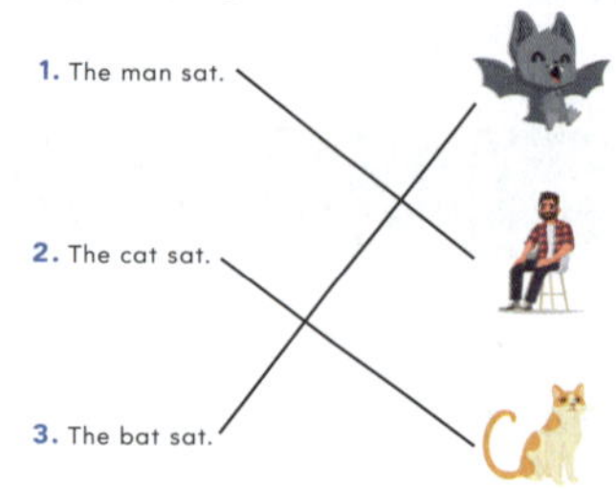

4. ran

Day 4 (page 21)

1. C
2. B
3. A
4. B

Day 5 (page 22)

Answers should complete the story in a logical way.

Unit 2

Week 1

Day 1 (page 23)

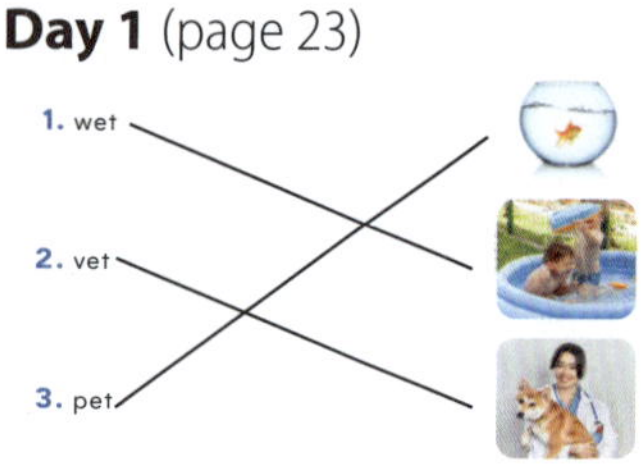

4. net

Day 2 (page 24)

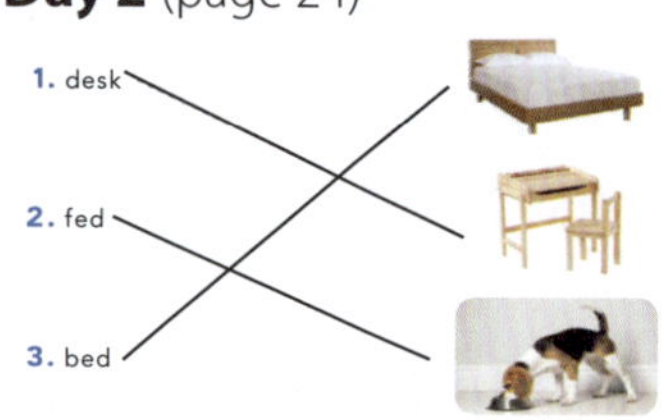

4. wreck

Day 3 (page 25)

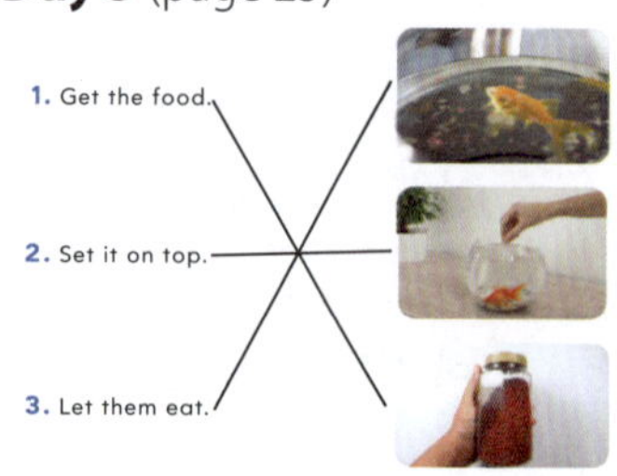

4. pets

Day 4 (page 27)

1. C
2. B
3. A
4. B

Day 5 (page 28)

Drawings should include a fish. Other objects that might be included are food, a shipwreck, and a shell.

Week 2

Day 1 (page 29)

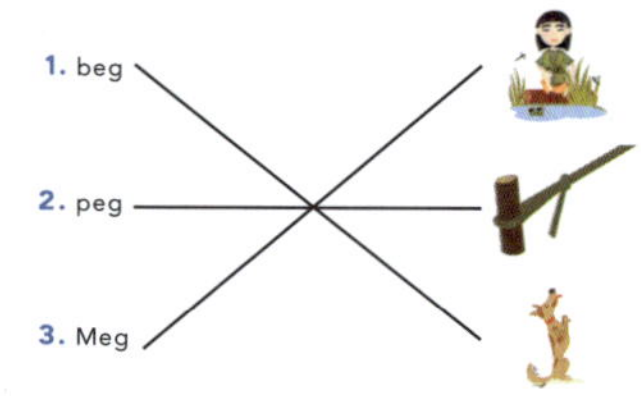

4. leg

Day 2 (page 30)

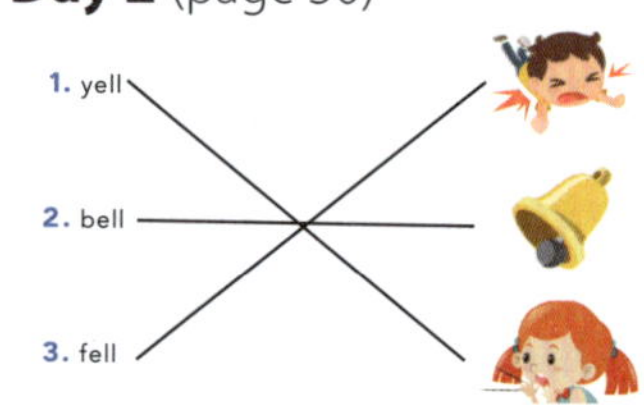

4. well

Day 3 (page 31)

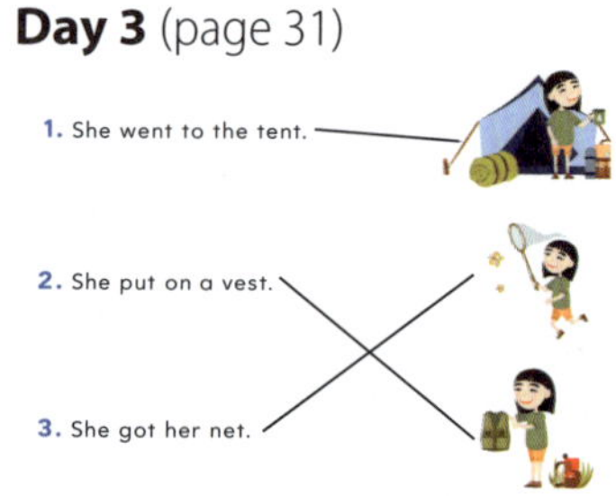

4. best

Day 4 (page 33)

1. A
2. B
3. B
4. C

Day 5 (page 34)

Answers should complete the story in a logical way.

Answer Key *(cont.)*

Unit 3

Week 1

Day 1 (page 35)

4. jig

Day 2 (page 36)

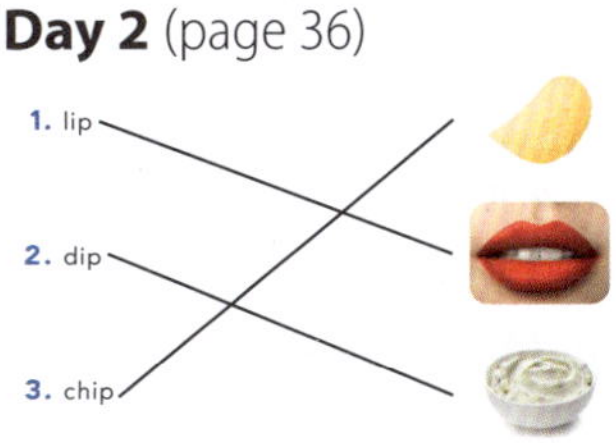

4. drip

Day 3 (page 37)

1. rig, dig
2. dig, pit
3. pick, dig
4. pig

Day 4 (page 39)

1. C
2. B
3. A
4. B

Day 5 (page 40)

The text is about things that dig. Drawings should include students digging.

Week 2

Day 1 (page 41)

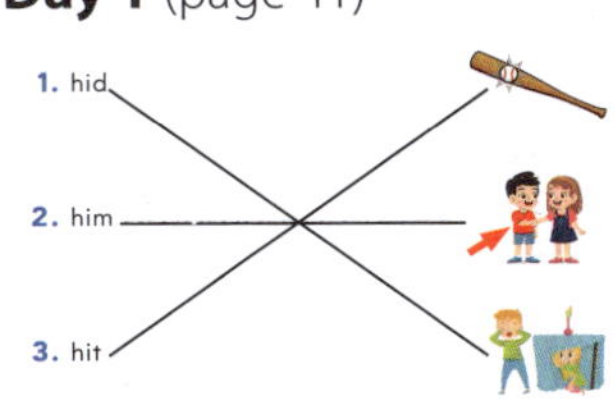

4. hip

Day 2 (page 42)

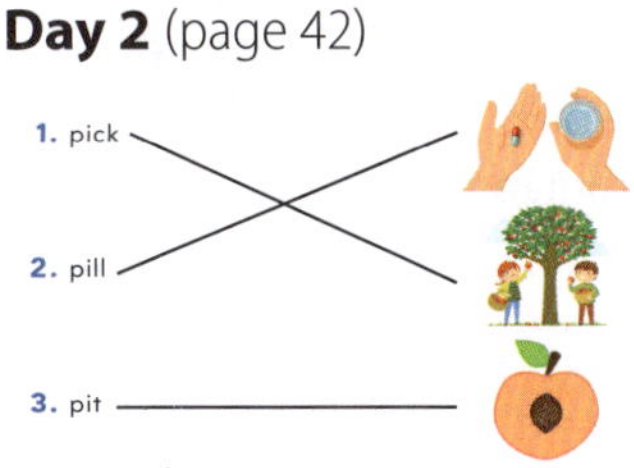

4. pin

Day 3 (page 43)

1. dig
2. stink
3. hid, sink
4. kiss

Day 4 (page 45)

1. A
2. B
3. A
4. B

Day 5 (page 46)

Answers should complete the story in a logical way.

Unit 4

Week 1

Day 1 (page 47)

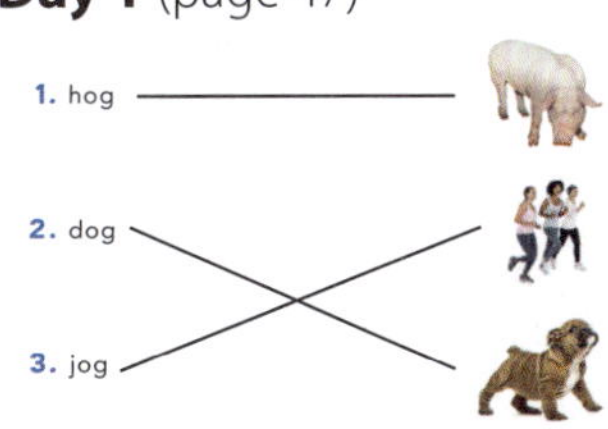

4. log

Day 2 (page 48)

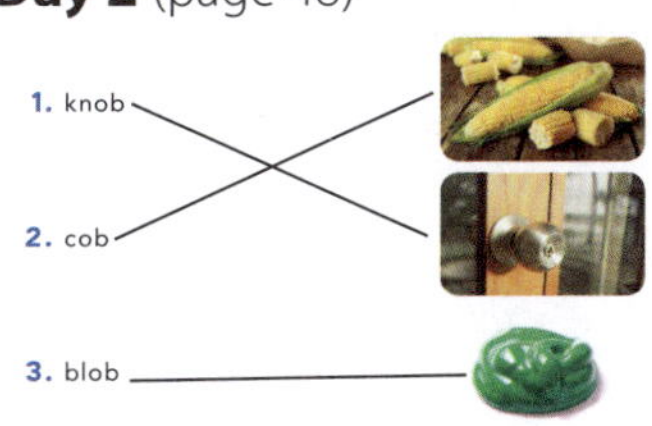

4. job

Day 3 (page 49)

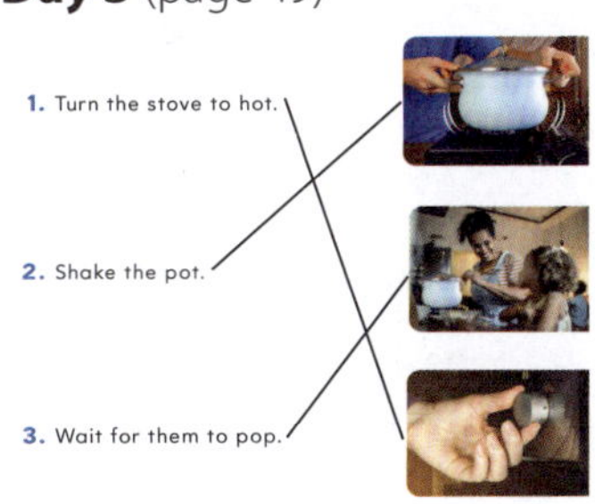

4. stove

Day 4 (page 51)

1. C
2. A
3. B
4. B

Day 5 (page 52)

Answers should should show the next logical step, such as eating popcorn or putting it in a bowl.

Week 2

Day 1 (page 53)

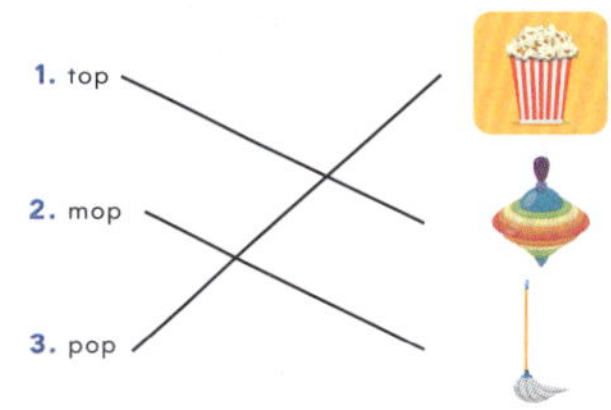

4. hop

Day 2 (page 54)

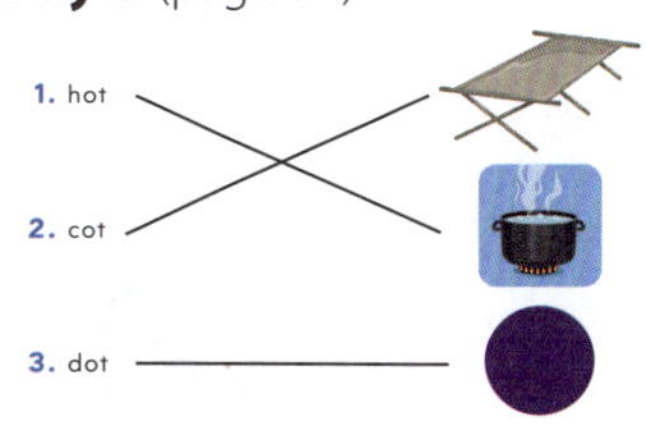

4. pot

Day 3 (page 55)

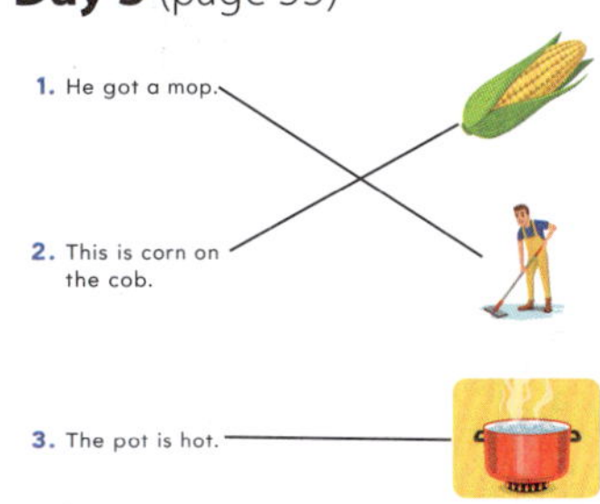

4. top

Day 4 (page 57)

1. C
2. A
3. B
4. A

Day 5 (page 58)

Answers should complete the story in a logical way.

Answer Key *(cont.)*

Unit 5

Week 1

Day 1 (page 59)

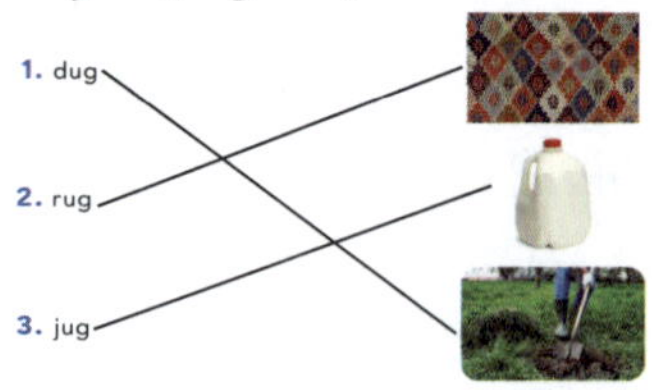

4. bug

Day 2 (page 60)

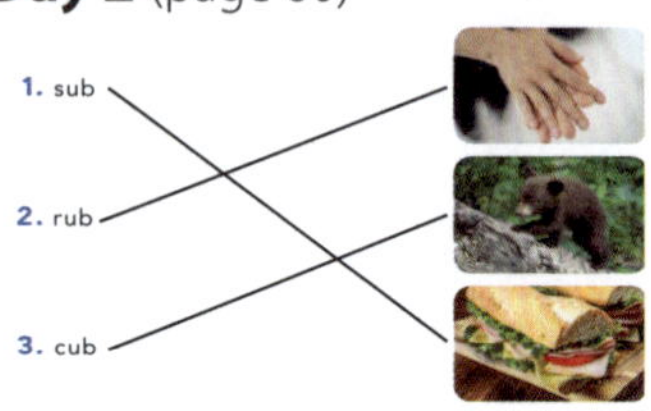

4. tub

Day 3 (page 61)

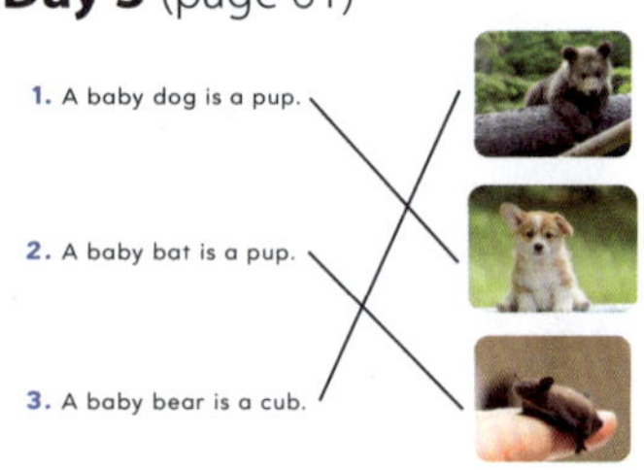

4. cub

Day 4 (page 63)

1. B
2. A
3. C
4. C

Day 5 (page 64)

Examples:
A baby mouse is a pup, too.
A baby tiger is a cub, too.

Week 2

Day 1 (page 65)

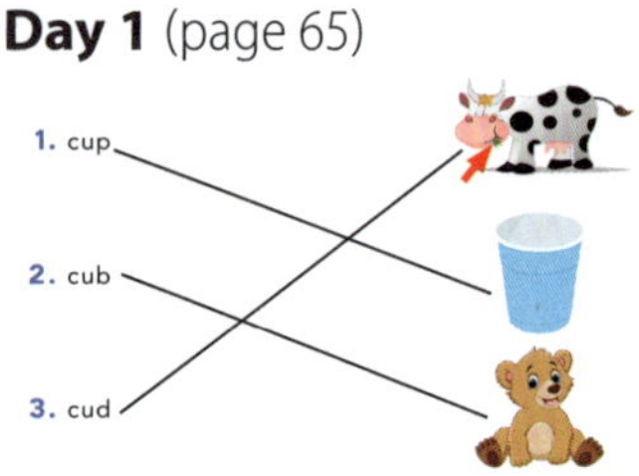

4. cut

Day 2 (page 66)

4. hut

Day 3 (page 67)

4. nut

Day 4 (page 69)

1. C
2. A
3. A
4. B

Day 5 (page 70)

Answers should complete the story in a logical way.

Unit 6

Week 1

Day 1 (page 71)

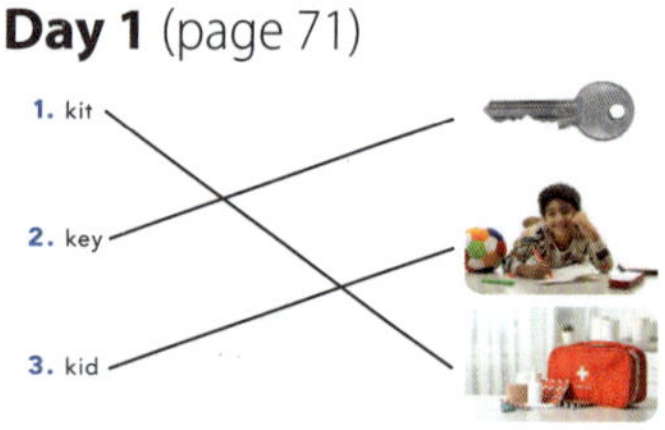

4. king

Day 2 (page 72)

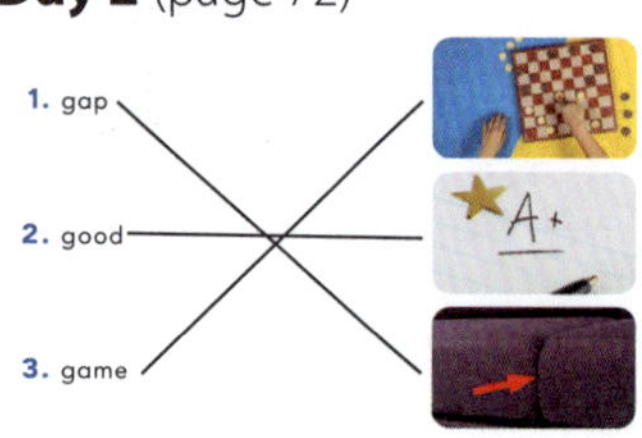

4. goat

Day 3 (page 73)

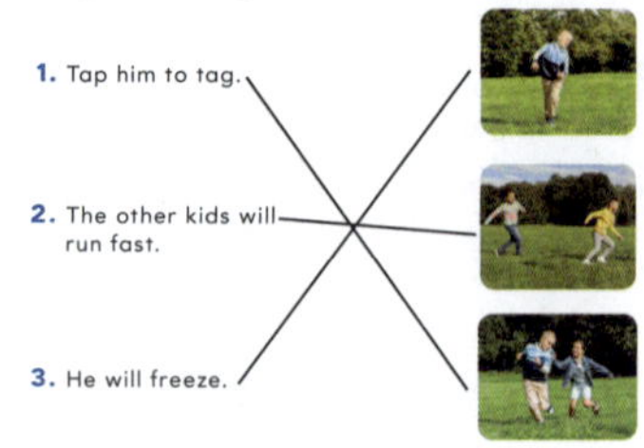

4. freeze

Day 4 (page 75)

1. A
2. B
3. B
4. B

Day 5 (page 76)

Answers should include a kid sitting down or standing still.

Week 2

Day 1 (page 77)

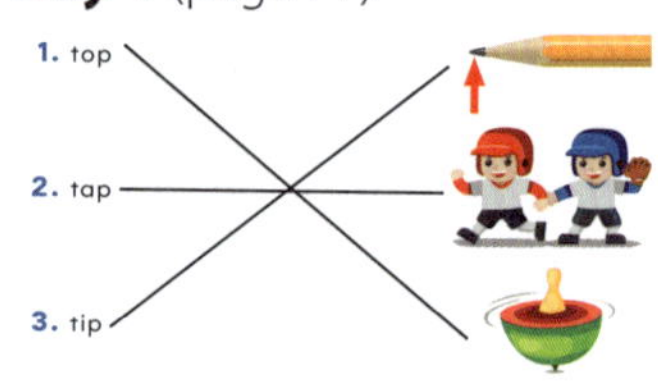

4. tag

Day 2 (page 78)

4. bug

Day 3 (page 79)

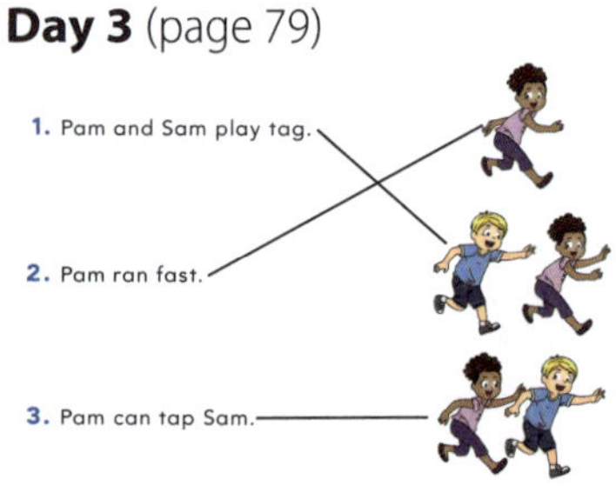

4. tag, tap

Answer Key *(cont.)*

Day 4 (page 81)

1. C **3.** B
2. B **4.** A

Day 5 (page 82)

Answers should include a labeled picture of Pam running away from Sam who is now it.

Unit 7

Week 1

Day 1 (page 83)

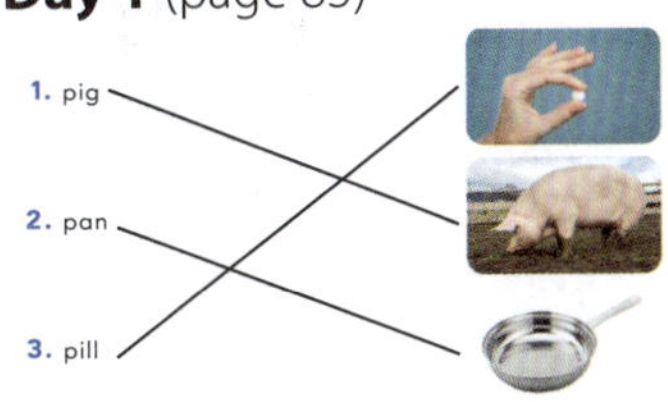

4. paw

Day 2 (page 84)

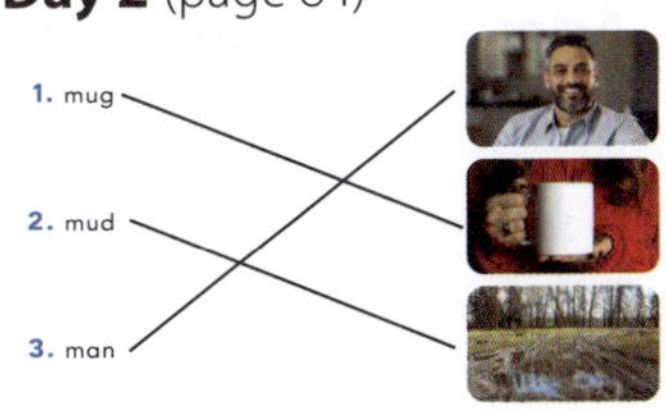

4. mail

Day 3 (page 85)

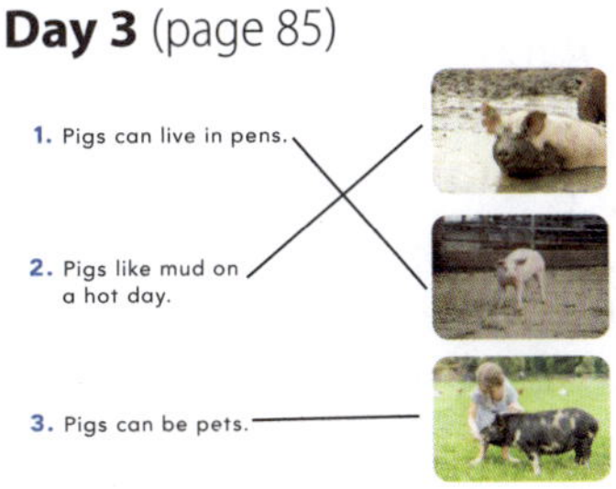

4. run, rug

Day 4 (page 87)

1. B **3.** C
2. A **4.** A

Day 5 (page 88)

Answers should show a fact from page 86.

Week 2

Day 1 (page 89)

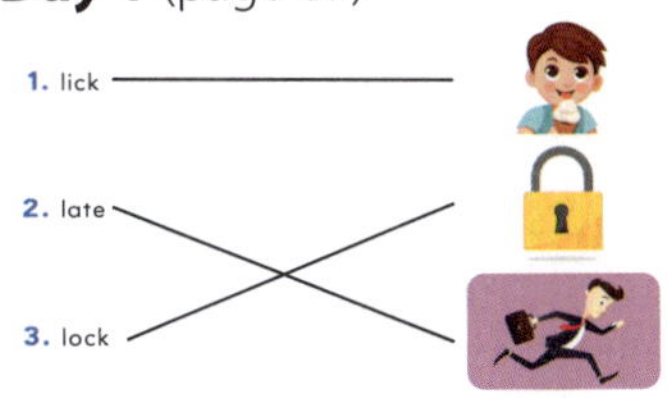

4. light

Day 2 (page 90)

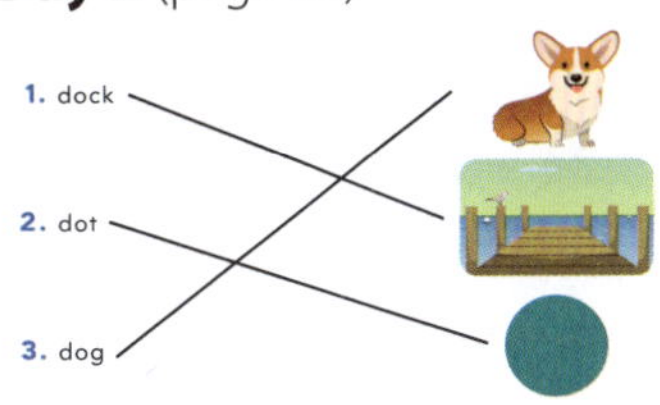

4. dice

Day 3 (page 91)

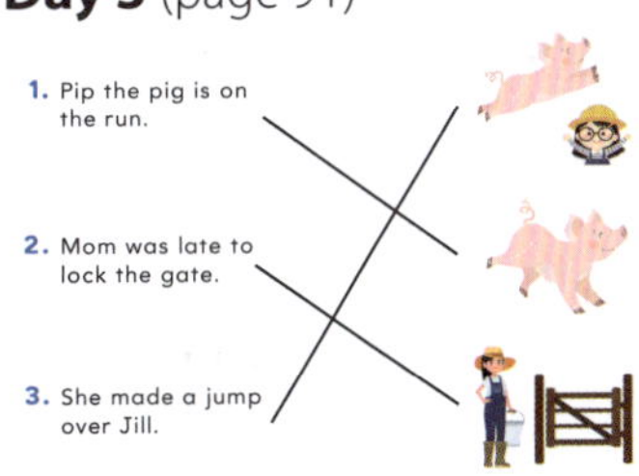

4. dog, den

Day 4 (page 93)

1. B **3.** B
2. C **4.** A

Day 5 (page 94)

Answers should include a drawing of Pip the pig inside the fenced area.

Unit 8

Week 1

Day 1 (page 95)

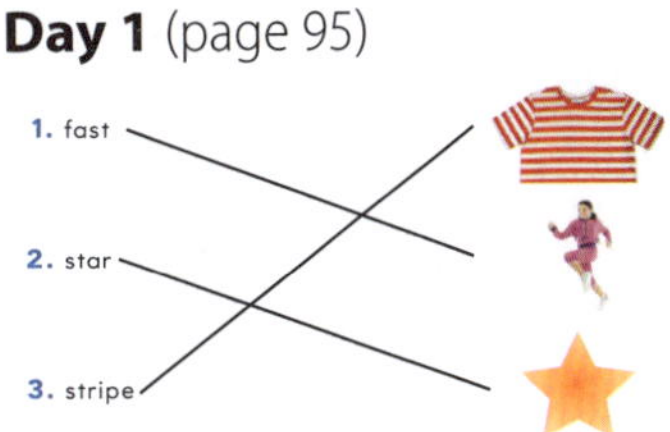

4. dust

Day 2 (page 96)

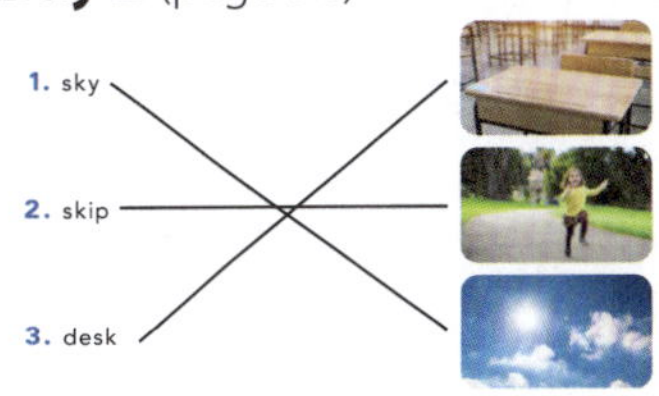

4. mask

Day 3 (page 97)

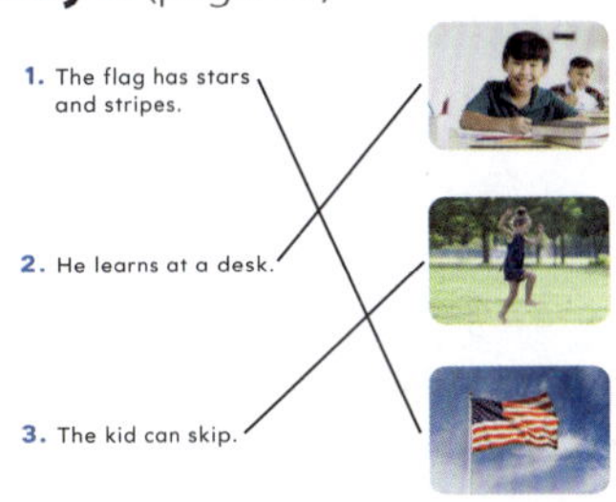

4. star

Day 4 (page 99)

1. A **3.** C
2. B **4.** C

Day 5 (page 100)

Answers should include a labeled drawing showing a flag in a classroom.

Week 2

Day 1 (page 101)

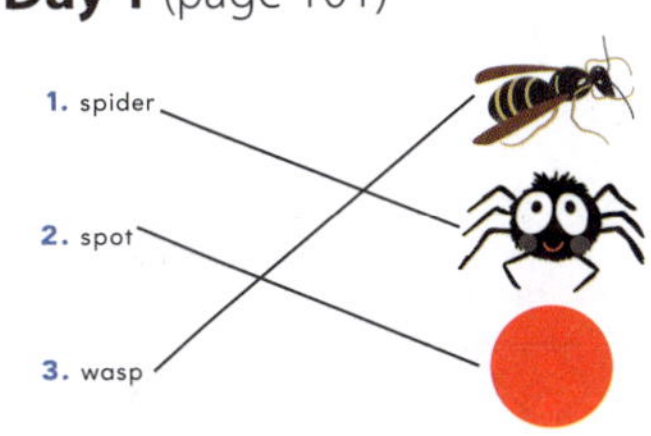

4. spy

Day 2 (page 102)

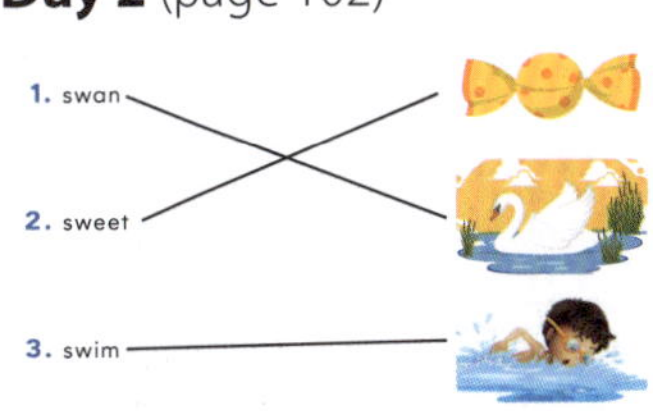

4. sweep

Answer Key *(cont.)*

Day 3 (page 103)

4. spider

Day 4 (page 105)

1. C
2. A
3. C
4. A

Day 5 (page 106)

Answers should include a labeled drawing of a child building a sandcastle at the beach.

Unit 9

Week 1

Day 1 (page 107)

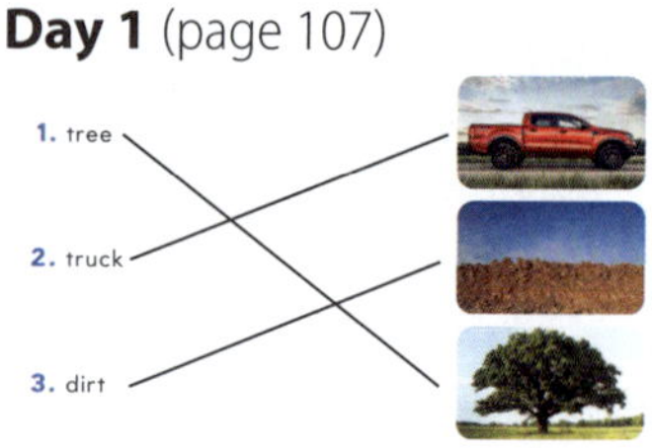

4. heart

Day 2 (page 108)

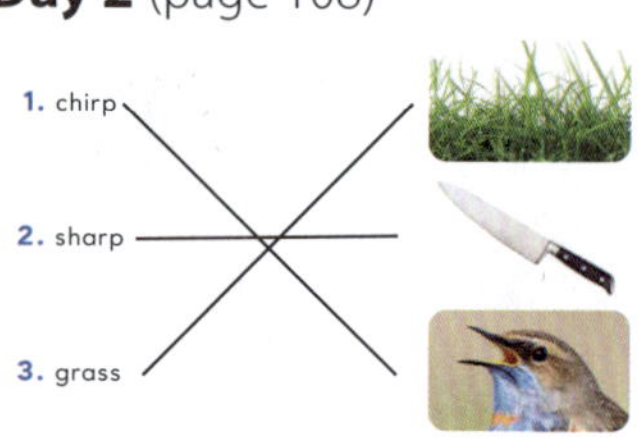

4. graze

Day 3 (page 109)

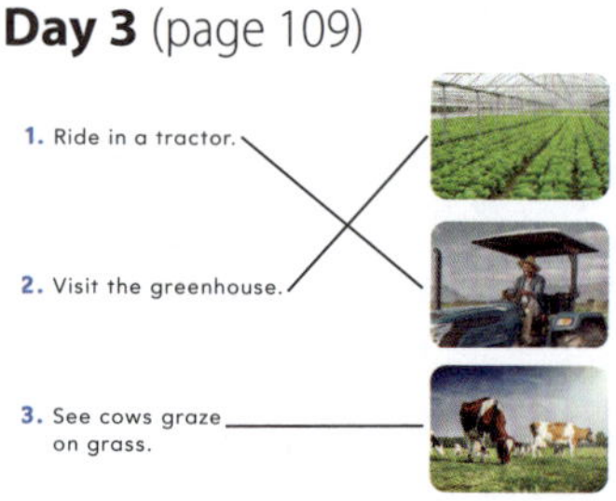

4. tree

Day 4 (page 111)

1. B
2. A
3. B
4. C

Day 5 (page 112)

Answers should include a labeled drawing of a child riding a tractor.

Week 2

Day 1 (page 113)

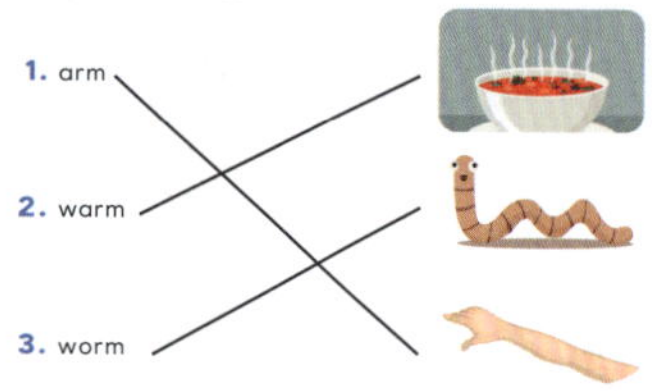

4. farm

Day 2 (page 114)

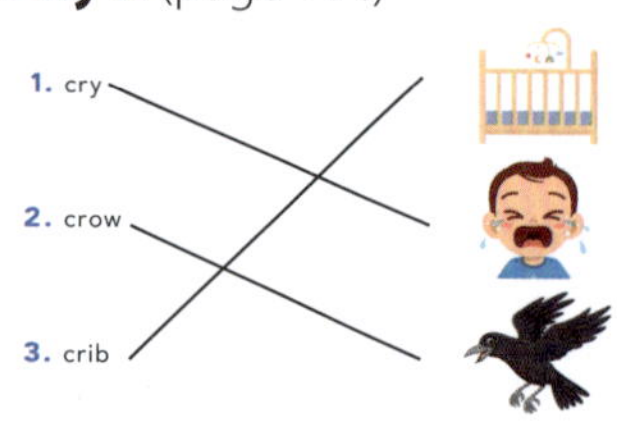

4. crash

Day 3 (page 115)

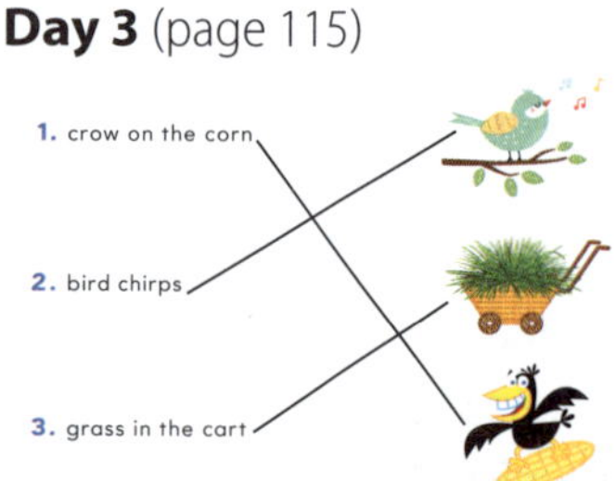

4. worm

Day 4 (page 117)

1. A
2. B
3. C
4. B

Day 5 (page 118)

Answers should include a drawing of a worm hiding deep in the dirt.

Unit 10

Week 1

Day 1 (page 119)

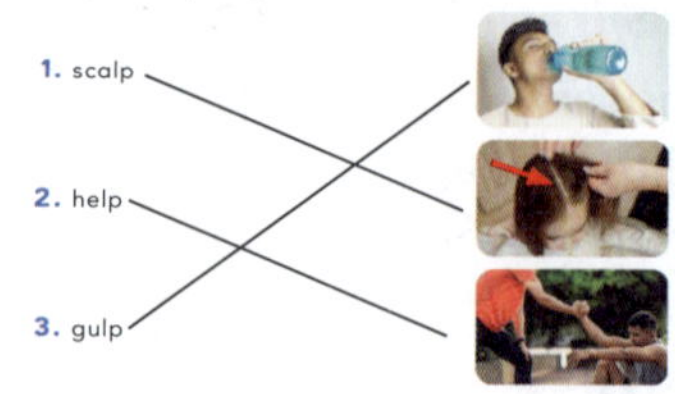

4. yelp

Day 2 (page 120)

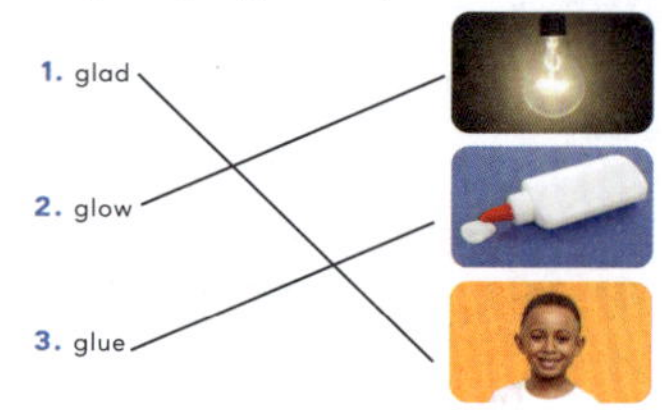

4. globe

Day 3 (page 121)

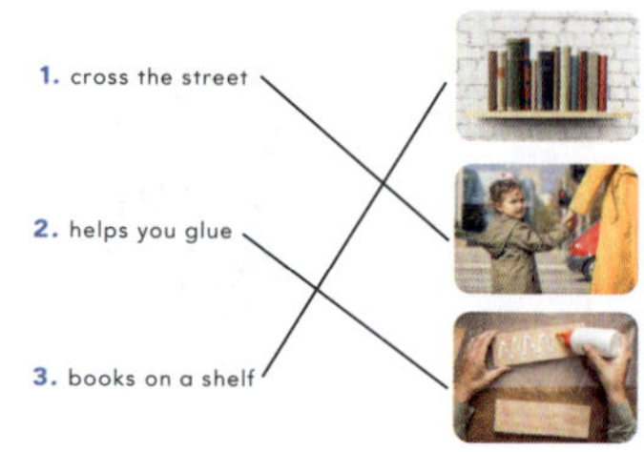

4. class, clean

Day 4 (page 123)

1. B
2. C
3. C
4. B

Day 5 (page 124)

Answers should include a drawing of school nurse and a sentence describing how the nurse helps, such as: A school nurse helps if you get hurt.

Week 2

Day 1 (page 125)

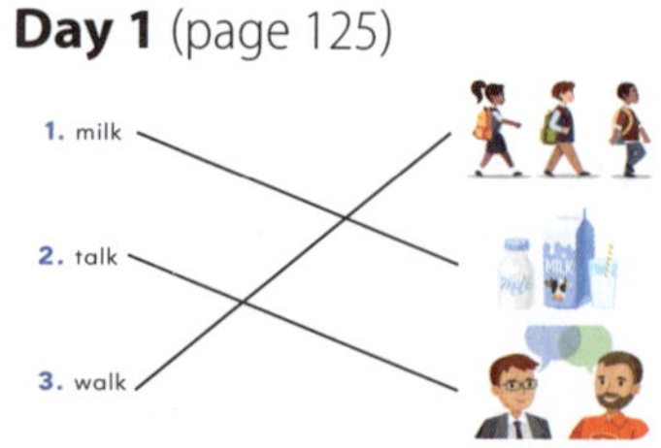

4. yolk

Answer Key *(cont.)*

Day 2 (page 126)

4. blink

Day 3 (page 127)

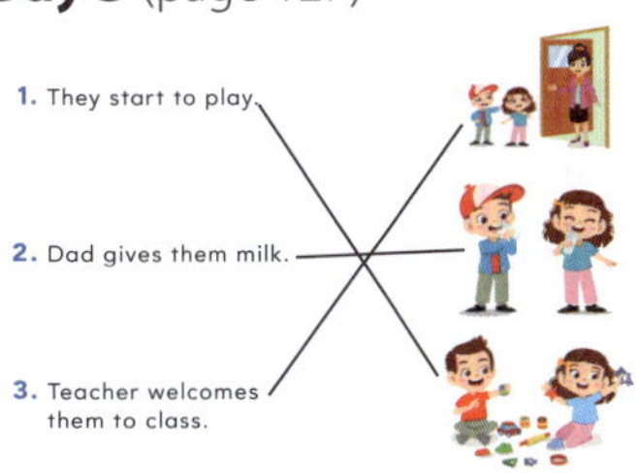

4. calf

Day 4 (page 129)

1. C	3. A
2. B	4. C

Day 5 (page 130)

Answers should include a drawing of a child who is late to class and a sentence describing why. Example includes: I was late because the car wouldn't start.

Unit 11

Week 1

Day 1 (page 131)

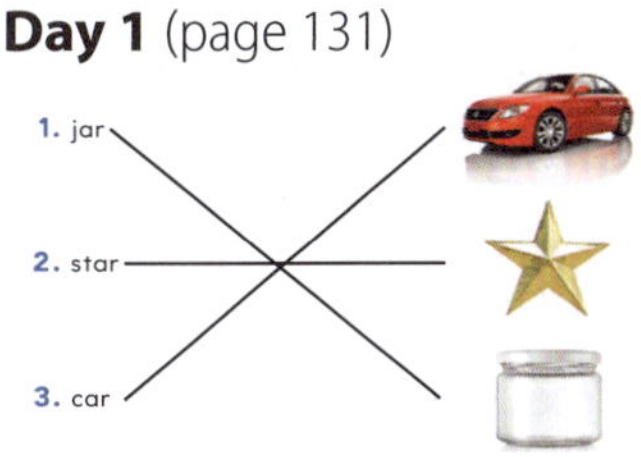

4. bar

Day 2 (page 132)

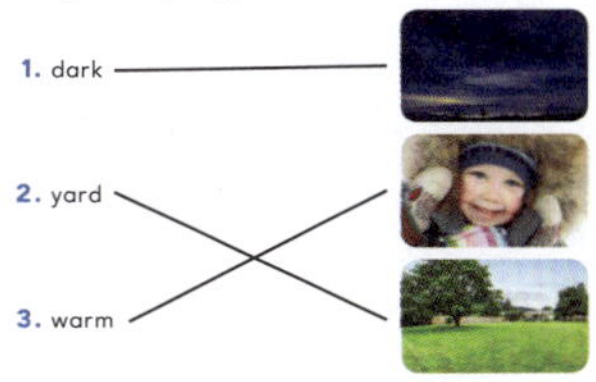

4. garden

Day 3 (page 133)

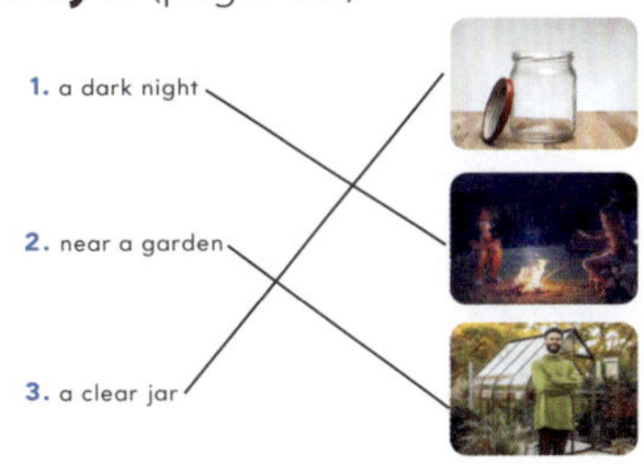

4. arm

Day 4 (page 135)

1. B	3. A
2. C	4. B

Day 5 (page 136)

Answers should include a drawing of someone catching fireflies using a flashlight covered in blue paper and a jar.

Week 2

Day 1 (page 137)

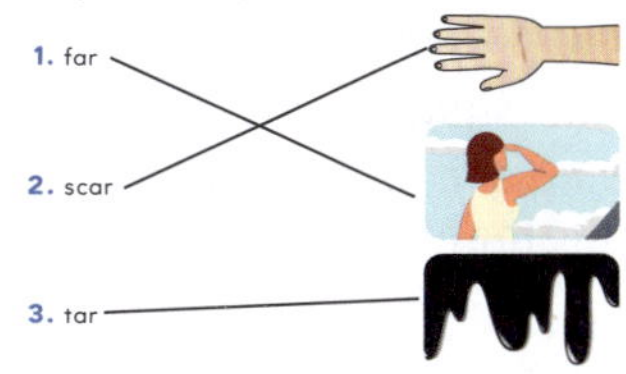

4. art

Day 2 (page 138)

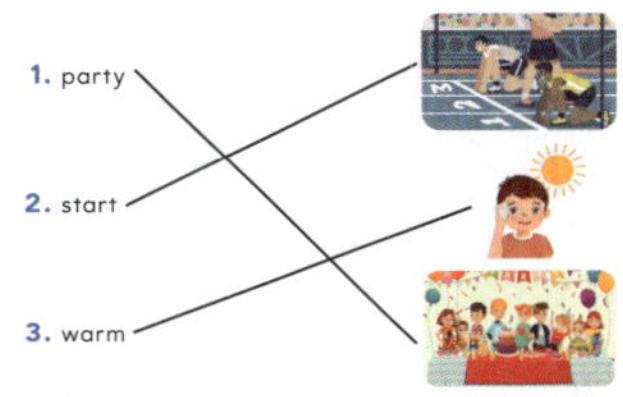

4. barn

Day 3 (page 139)

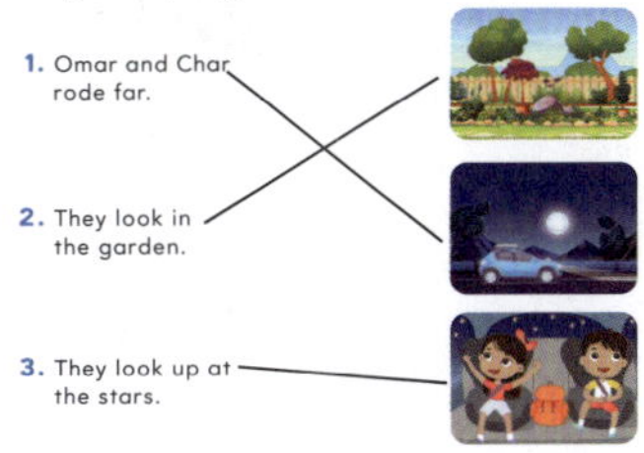

4. shark

Day 4 (page 141)

1. B	3. B
2. A	4. C

Day 5 (page 142)

Answers should include a drawing of two children catching fireflies.

Unit 12

Week 1

Day 1 (page 143)

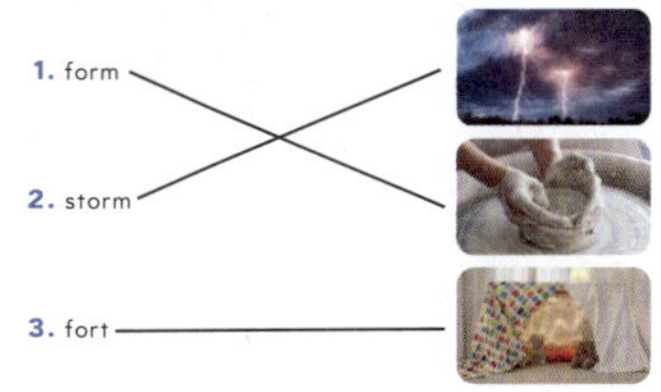

4. horn

Day 2 (page 144)

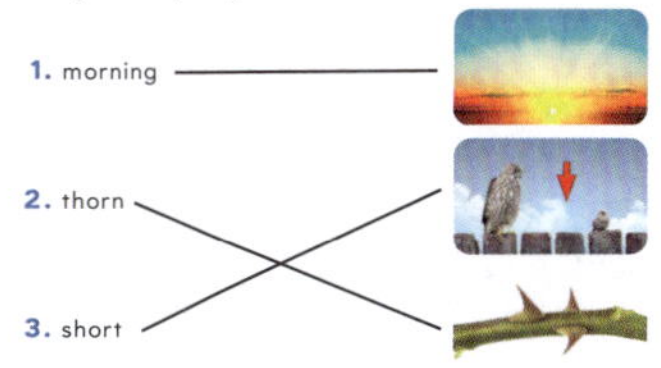

4. cork

Day 3 (page 145)

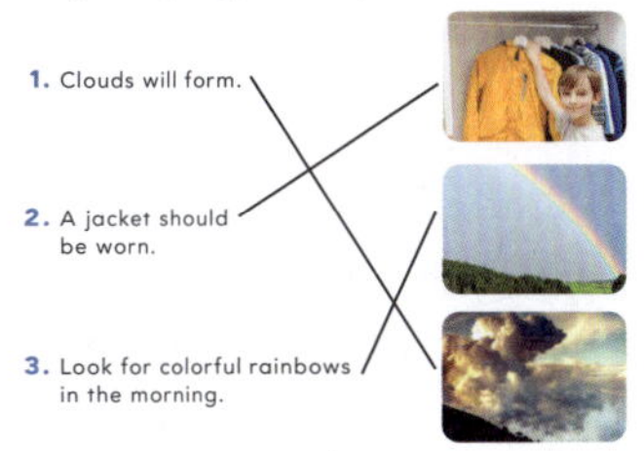

4. short, storm

Day 4 (page 147)

1. C	3. A
2. A	4. C

Day 5 (page 148)

Answers should include labeled drawings of what children will wear on Wednesday.

Answer Key *(cont.)*

Week 2

Day 1 (page 149)

4. door

Day 2 (page 150)

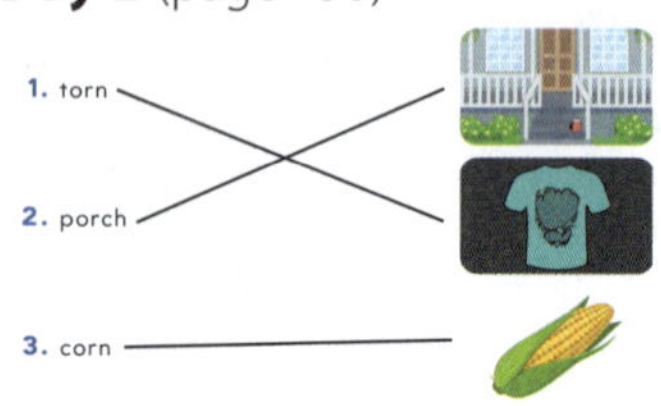

4. sword

Day 3 (page 151)

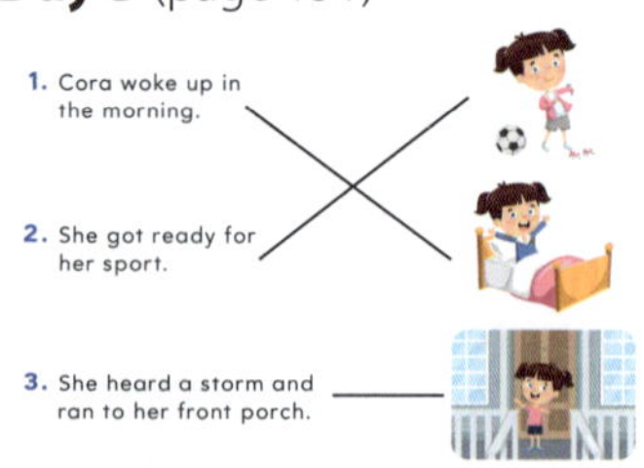

4. door

Day 4 (page 153)

1. C	**3.** A
2. B	**4.** B

Day 5 (page 154)

Answers should include a drawing of Cora jumping in the puddles.

Unit 13

Week 1

Day 1 (page 155)

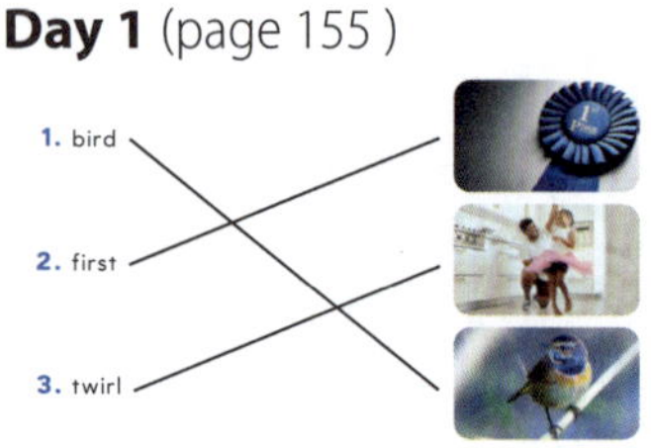

4. skirt

Day 2 (page 156)

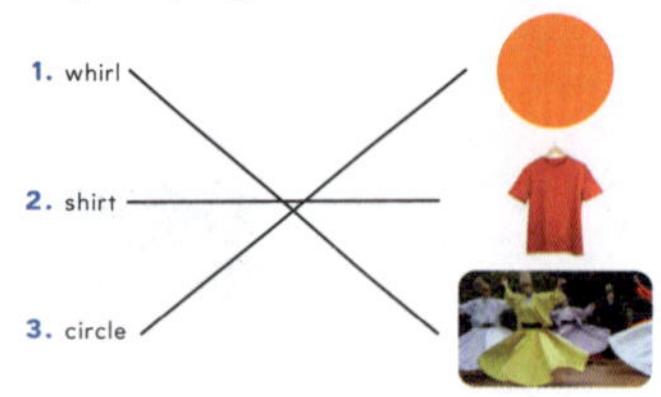

4. dirty

Day 3 (page 157)

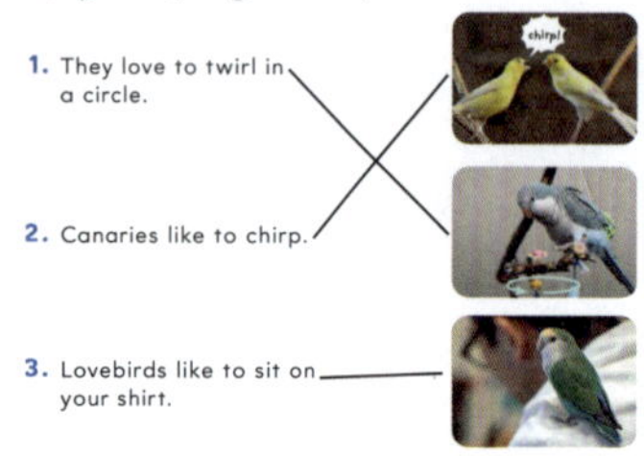

4. first

Day 4 (page 159)

1. C	**3.** A
2. B	**4.** A

Day 5 (page 160)

Answers should include a drawing of a bird the student would choose as a pet.

Week 2

Day 1 (page 161)

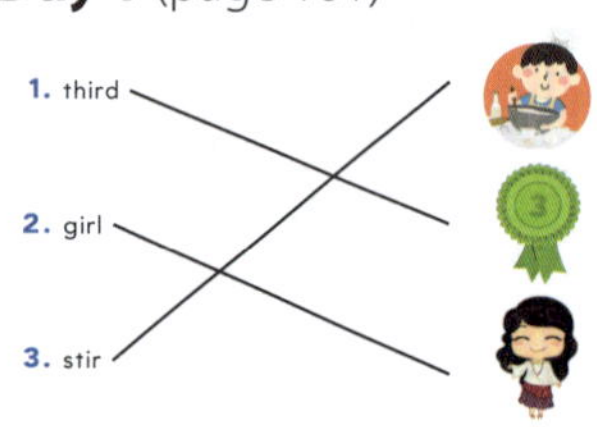

4. circus

Day 2 (page 162)

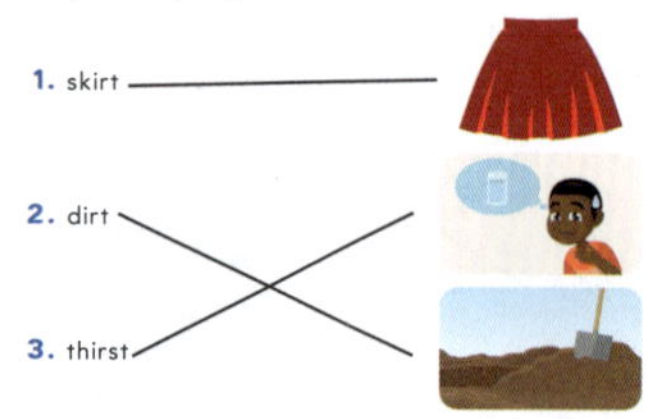

4. tired

Day 3 (page 163)

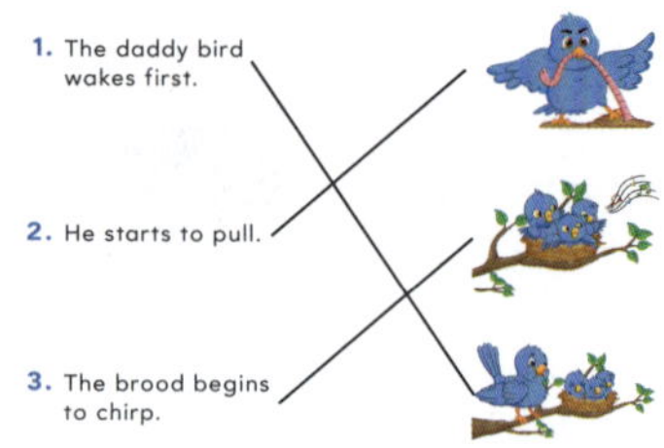

4. squirmy

Day 4 (page 165)

1. B	**3.** A
2. B	**4.** B

Day 5 (page 166)

Answers should include the dad bird going to get more worms.

Unit 14

Week 1

Day 1 (page 167)

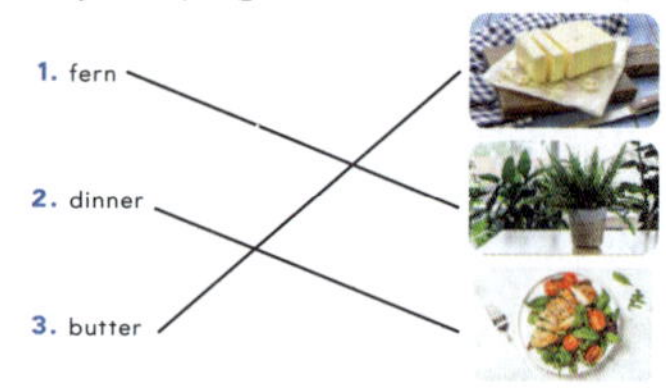

4. herd

Day 2 (page 168)

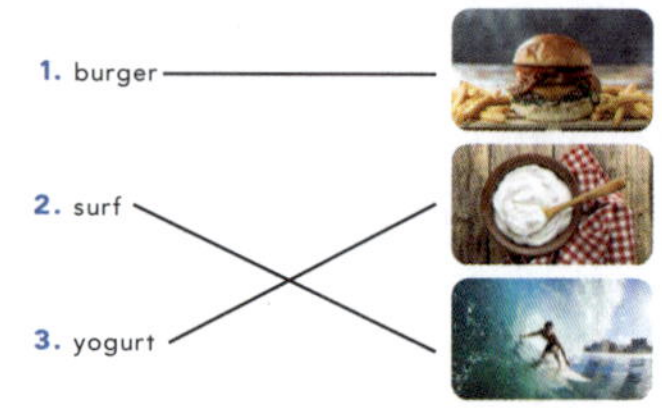

4. burn

Day 3 (page 169)

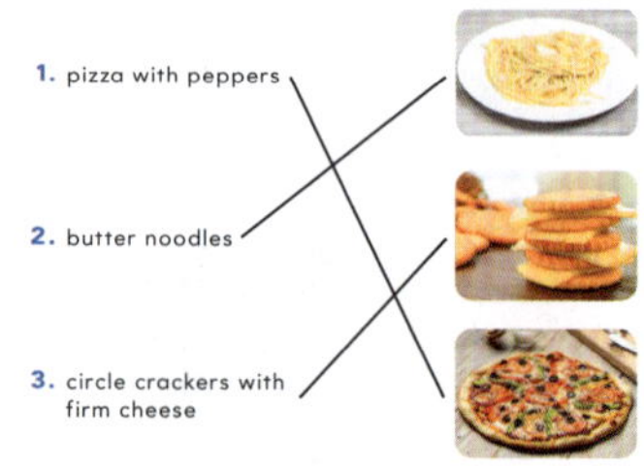

4. burger

Answer Key *(cont.)*

Day 4 (page 171)

1. C **3.** A
2. A **4.** B

Day 5 (page 172)

Answers should include a labeled drawing of pizza with peppers.

Week 2

Day 1 (page 173)

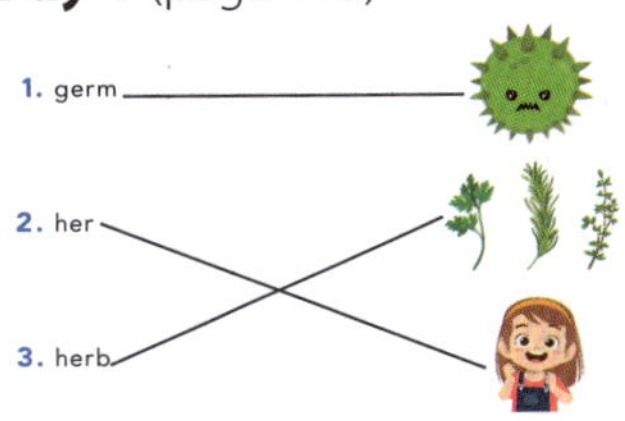

4. over

Day 2 (page 174)

4. purr

Day 3 (page 175)

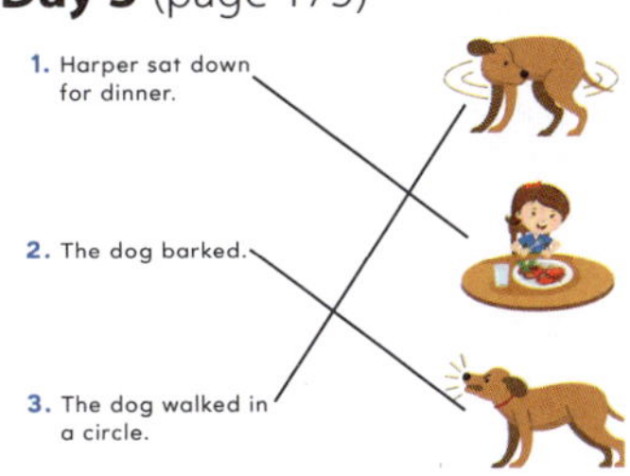

4. dinner

Day 4 (page 177)

1. A **3.** C
2. B **4.** A

Day 5 (page 178)

Answers should include a drawing of the dog eating his own dinner and the sentence: Murry gave up and ate his mush.

Unit 15

Week 1

Day 1 (page 179)

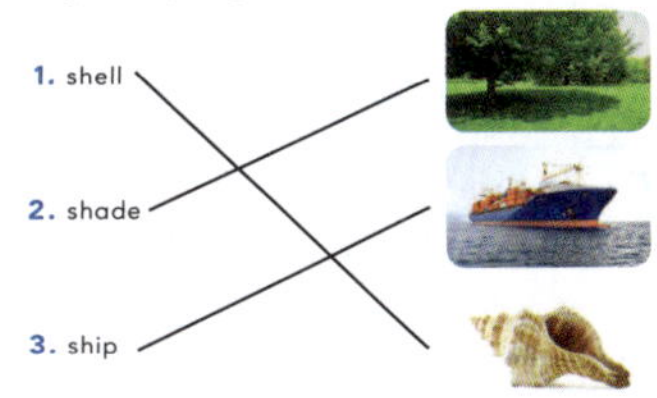

4. show

Day 2 (page 180)

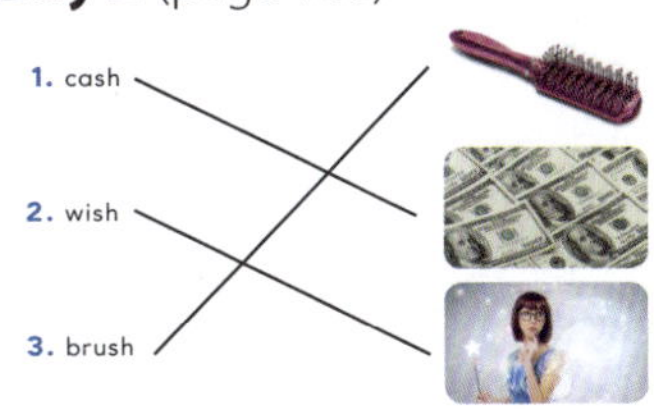

4. trash

Day 3 (page 181)

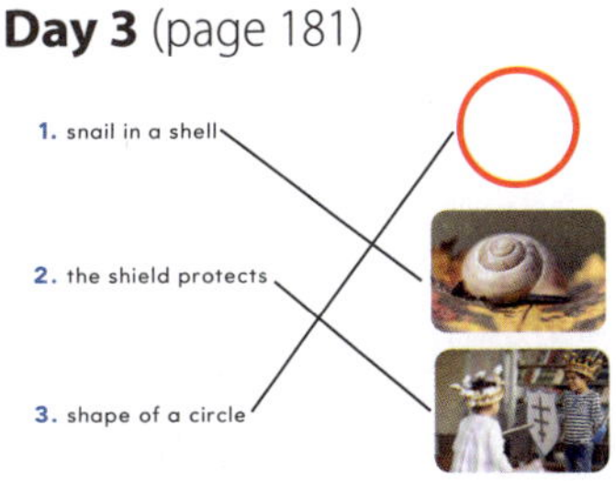

4. shrubs

Day 4 (page 183)

1. B **3.** B
2. A **4.** C

Day 5 (page 184)

Answers should include a drawing of a turtle and the sentence: A turtle will hide in the shell if it is scared.

Week 2

Day 1 (page 185)

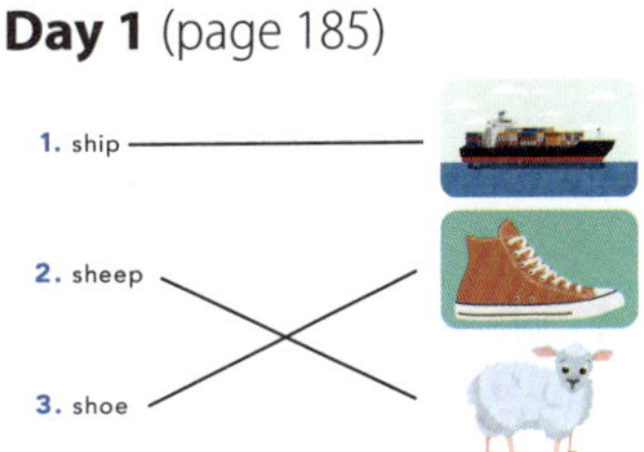

4. shelf

Day 2 (page 186)

4. lash

Day 3 (page 187)

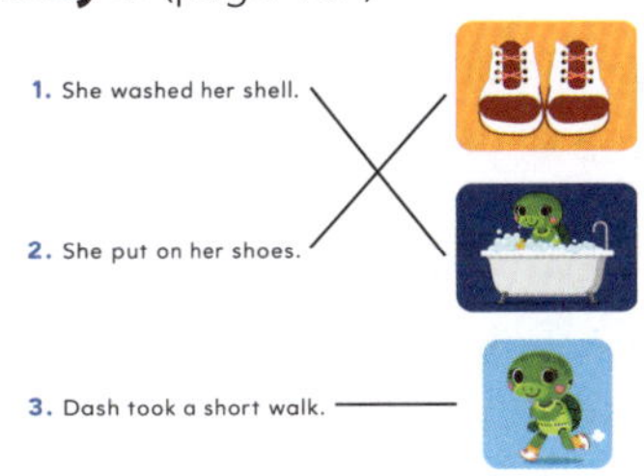

4. shore

Day 4 (page 189)

1. B **3.** A
2. C **4.** C

Day 5 (page 190)

Answers should include a drawing the turtle celebrating after winning the race and the sentence: Dash did it!

Unit 16

Week 1

Day 1 (page 191)

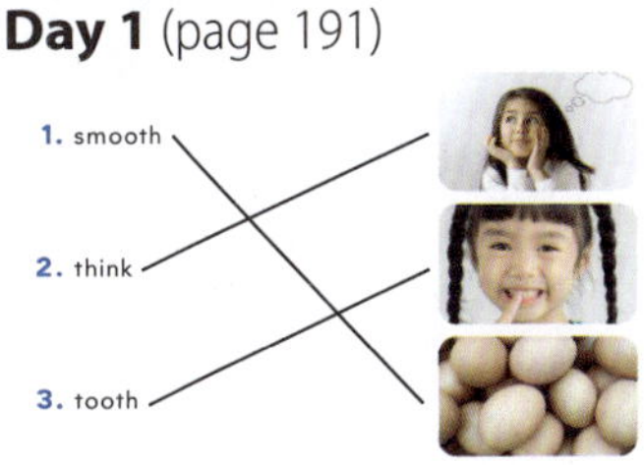

4. thread

Day 2 (page 192)

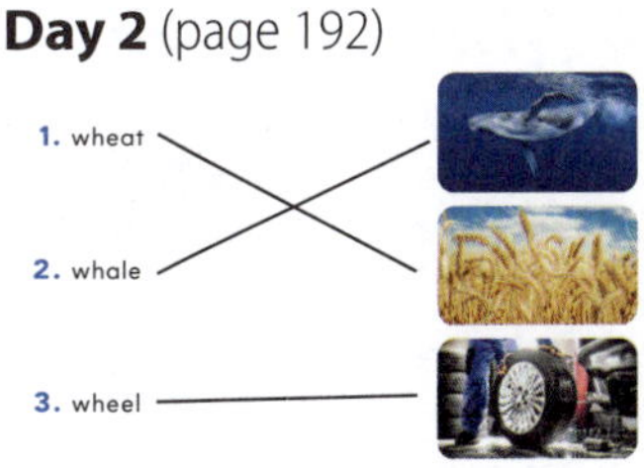

4. whisk

Answer Key *(cont.)*

Day 3 (page 193)

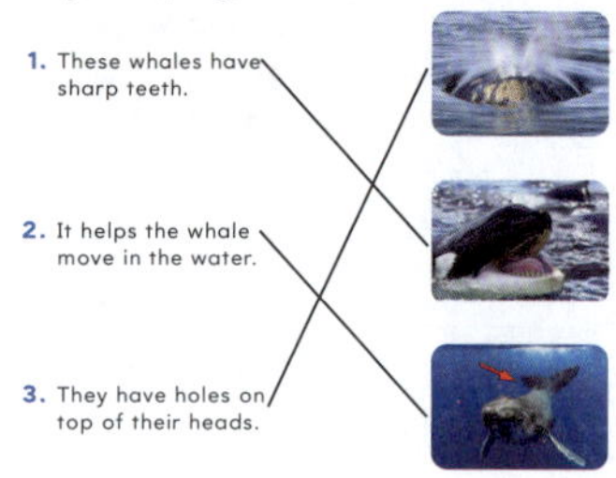

4. whales

Day 4 (page 195)

1. B **3.** A
2. C **4.** C

Day 5 (page 196)

Answers should include a labeled drawing of a whale including baleen or teeth, blow hole, tail, and head.

Week 2

Day 1 (page 197)

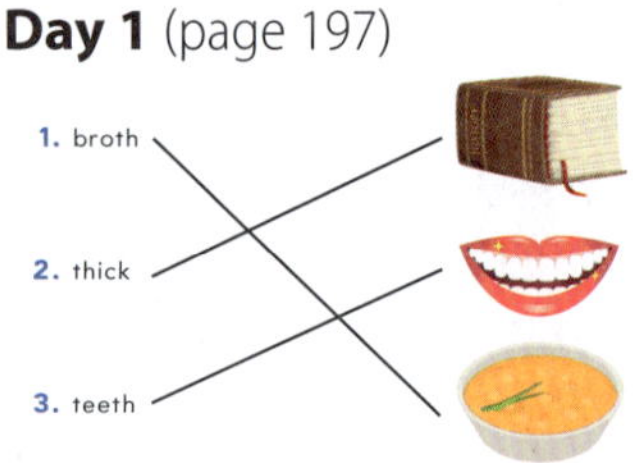

4. moth

Day 2 (page 198)

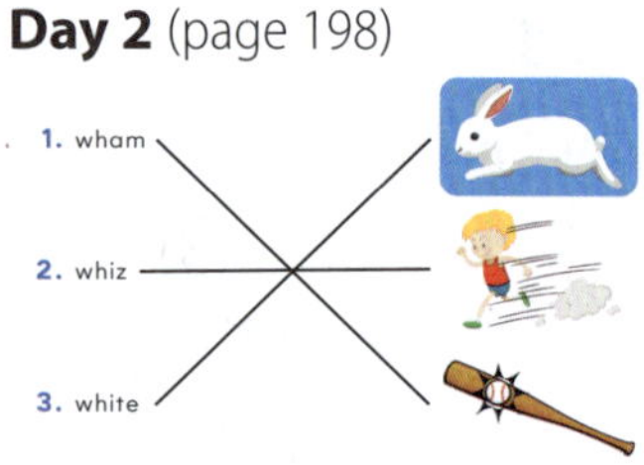

4. why

Day 3 (page 199)

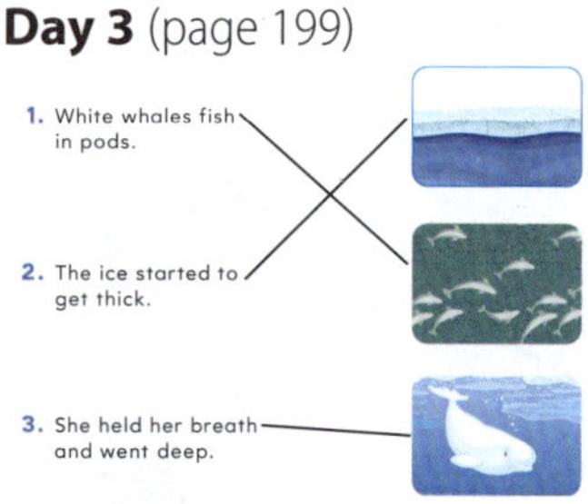

4. both

Day 4 (page 201)

1. B **3.** A
2. C **4.** C

Day 5 (page 202)

Answers should include a drawing of Whit reunited with her mom and dad and the sentence: Whit found her mom and dad.

Unit 17

Week 1

Day 1 (page 203)

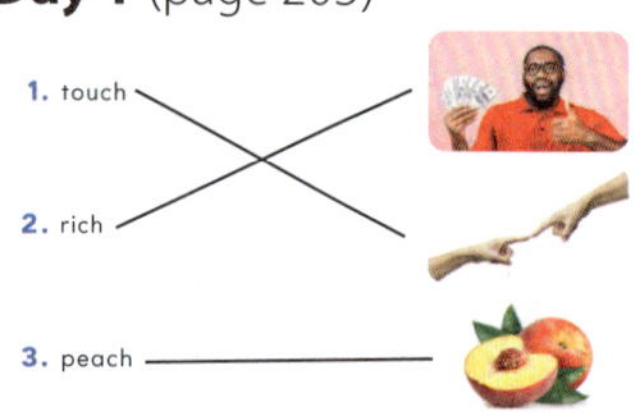

4. branch

Day 2 (page 204)

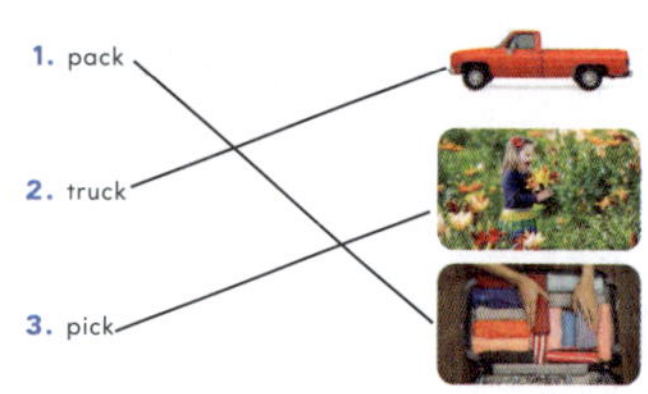

4. sticky

Day 3 (page 205)

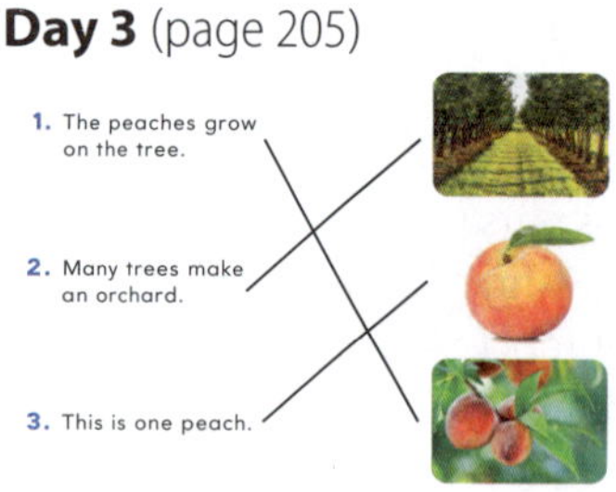

4. sticky

Day 4 (page 207)

1. B **3.** C
2. A **4.** A

Day 5 (page 208)

Answers should include a drawing of peaches packed in a truck.

Week 2

Day 1 (page 209)

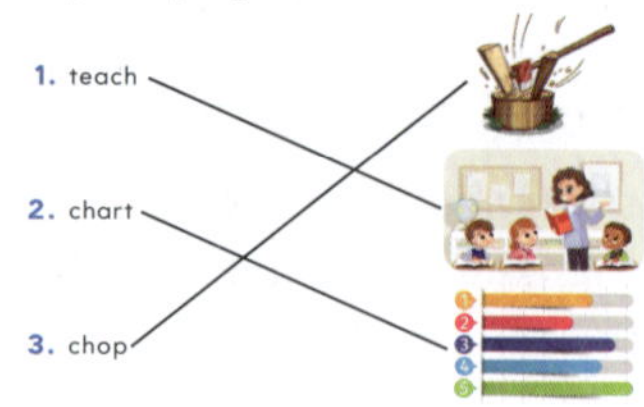

4. chin

Day 2 (page 210)

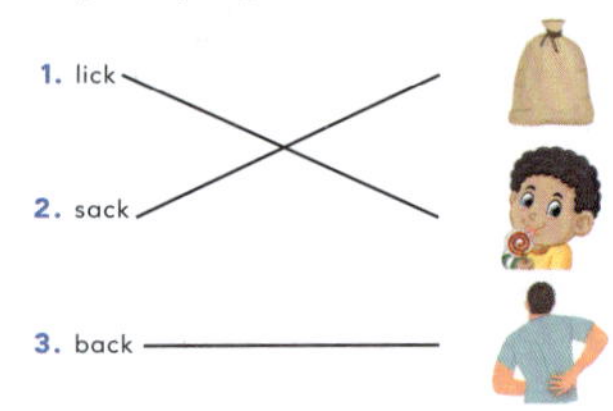

4. neck

Day 3 (page 211)

Day 4 (page 213)

1. C **3.** A
2. B **4.** A

Day 5 (page 214)

Answers should include a drawing of Charlie serving pieces of pie to his friends and the sentence: Everyone liked eating the pies.

Answer Key *(cont.)*

Unit 18

Week 1

Day 1 (page 215)

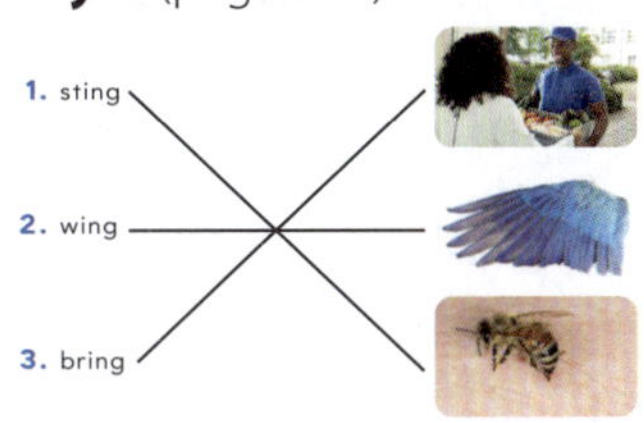

4. wring

Day 2 (page 216)

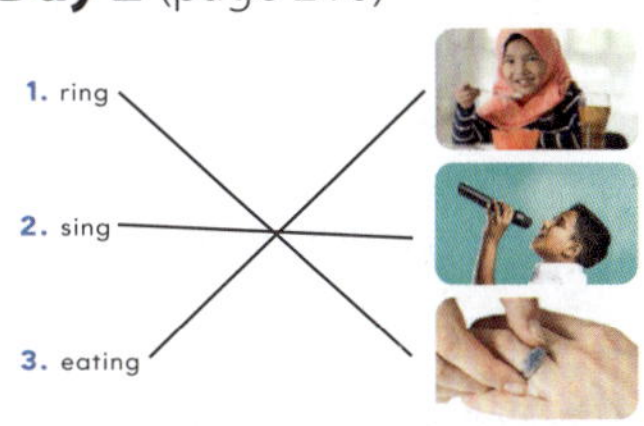

4. swing

Day 3 (page 217)

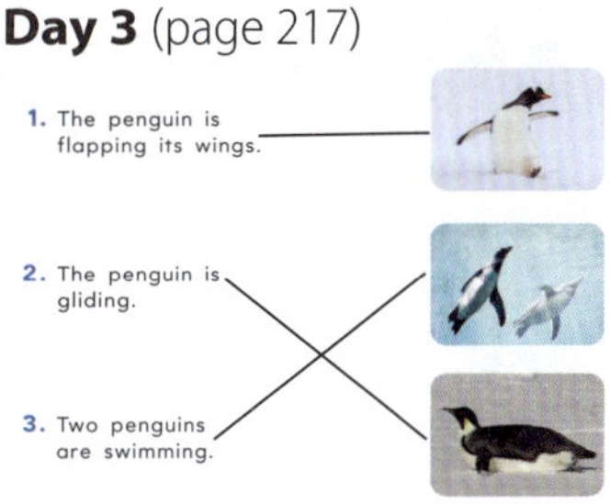

4. wings

Day 4 (page 219)

1. A
2. A
3. C
4. C

Day 5 (page 220)

Answers should include a drawing of a bat and the sentence: I like bats because they can hang upside down.

Week 2

Day 1 (page 221)

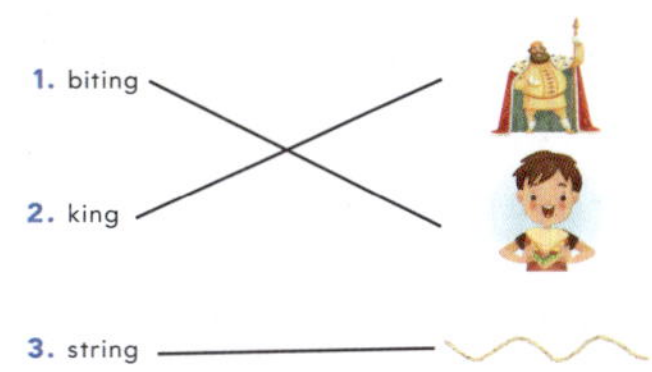

4. licking

Day 2 (page 222)

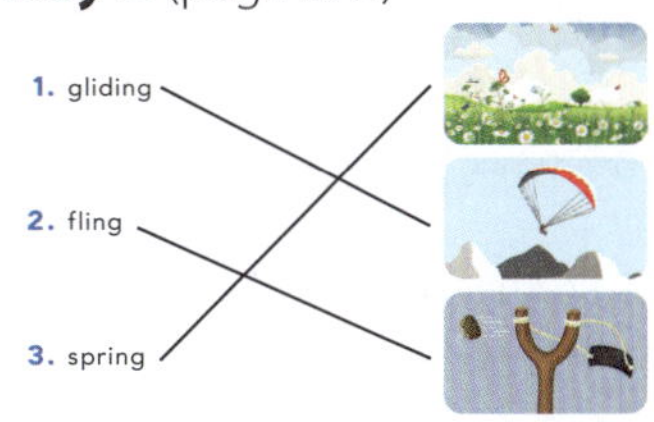

4. swimming

Day 3 (page 223)

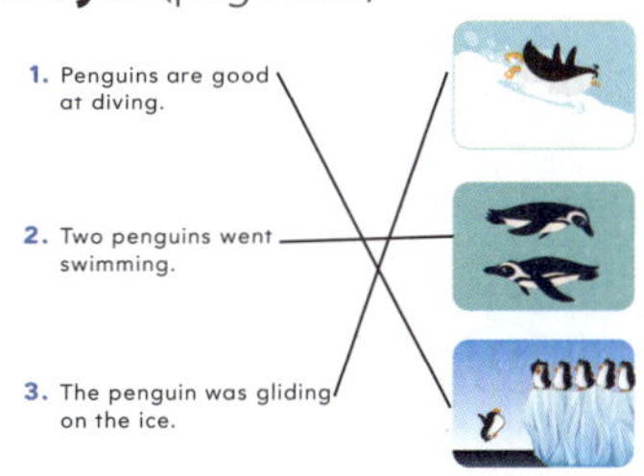

4. king

Day 4 (page 225)

1. A
2. B
3. B
4. A

Day 5 (page 226)

Answers should include a drawing of Ling joining the other penguins in playing and gliding and the sentence: Ling joined the other penguins playing.

Digital Resources

Accessing the Digital Resources

The digital resources can be downloaded by following these steps:

1. Go to **www.tcmpub.com/digital**
2. Use the 13-digit ISBN number to redeem the digital resources.
3. Respond to the question using the book.
4. Follow the prompts on the Content Cloud website to sign in or create a new account.
5. The content redeemed will appear on your My Content screen. Click on the product to look through the digital resources. All file resources are available for download. Select files can be previewed, opened, and shared.

For questions and assistance with your ISBN redemption, please contact Shell Education.

email: customerservice@tcmpub.com

phone: 800-858-7339

Contents of the Digital Resources

- Standards Correlations
- Writing Rubric
- Fluency Rubric
- Class and Individual Analysis Sheets

